DISCOVER · NATURE

close to Home

DISCOVER · NATURE

close to Home

Things to Know and Things to Do

Elizabeth P. Lawlor

with illustrations by Pat Archer

STACKPOLE
BOOKS

Published by
STACKPOLE BOOKS
Cameron and Kelker Streets
P.O. Box 1831
Harrisburg, PA 17105

Printed in the United States of America

Cover illustrations by Pat Archer
Cover design by Mark Olszewski with Christine Mercer

First Edition

10 9 8 7 6 5 4

Library of Congress Cataloging-in-Publication Data

Lawlor, Elizabeth P.
    Discover nature close to home : things to know and things to do /
Elizabeth P. Lawlor ; with illustrations by Pat Archer. — 1st ed.
        p.   cm.
    Includes bibliographical references
    Summary: Introduces the three zones of our backyard environment,
the canopy, field, and forest floor, and describes the plant and
animal life found there. Includes simple experiments and activities.
    ISBN 0-8117-3077-8 : $14.95
    1. Forest fauna—Juvenile literature.   2. Forest flora—Juvenile
literature.   3. Plant canopies—Juvenile literature.   4. Nature
study—Juvenile literature. [1. Forest animals.   2. Forest plants.
3. Nature study.]   I. Archer, Pat, ill.   II. Title
QH86.L39   1993
508—dc20   92–36401
                                                              CIP
                                                               AC

To Agnes and Sarah
with love

Only
look
. . . . and
someday
you
will
see.

Anthony DeMello, S.J.
Wellsprings

TABLE OF CONTENTS

PART III: THE FOREST FLOOR

ACKNOWLEDGMENTS

I am indebted to many scientists, field researchers, and authors whose work has made this book possible. I am especially grateful, however, to the science specialists who took time from their busy schedules to review my work: Dr. Graeme Berlyn, Yale University, School of Forestry and Environmental Studies; Dr. David Farr, National Fungus Collection, United States Department of Agriculture; Mr. Nathan Irwin, Insect Zoo, Smithsonian Institution, Washington, D.C.; Ms. Catherine Meehan, Horticulture Services Division, Smithsonian Institution; Sherry K. Pittam, Botany Department, Smithsonian Institution.

I also want to thank Stackpole Books editors Sally Atwater and Duane Gerlach for their patience and guidance.

Other reviewers who read parts of the manuscript and offered helpful suggestions were Lauren Brown, author and director of adult education for the Connecticut Audubon Society, Fairfield, Connecticut; Ted Gilman, environmental specialist, National Audubon Society Center, Greenwich, Connecticut; Marianne Smith, curator of natural sciences, Bruce Museum, Greenwich, Connecticut.

These acknowledgments would not be complete without recognition of two special friends: David A. Laux, Jr., who could always be counted on to find an uncommon lichen or a cluster of well-hidden spider egg sacs, and his sister, Louise Elizabeth Laux, who was always an enthusiastic companion on our forays into the woodlands.

Introduction

This book, the second in the Discover Nature series, is for people who want to find out about the plants and animals that live close to us. Like the first volume in the series, this book is concerned with knowing and doing. It is for the young, for parents, for students, for teachers, for retirees, for all those with a new or renewed interest in the world around us. Getting started as a naturalist requires a friendly, patient guide. This book is intended to be just that.

Each chapter introduces you to a common, easily found plant or animal. You will learn about its unique place in the web of life and the most fascinating aspects of its life-style. Each chapter also provides you with activities, things you can do to discover for yourself where to find each living thing, what it looks like, and how it behaves and survives.

Start with any part or chapter in this book. For instance, if you are taking a vacation to the North Woods, begin reading about cone-bearing evergreens, squirrels, and chipmunks, and pack the items suggested in the second part of each chapter. Consider keeping a field notebook.

My hope is that this book is only a beginning for you. When you have gone into the woods, into fields or meadows, or into your own backyard, and when you have experienced these places throughout the year, you have gone beyond all the books. Once you have started, you will have the best guide of all, Nature herself.

WHAT TO BRING

To become fully involved in the hands-on activities suggested in this book, you'll need very little equipment. Your basic kit requires only a few essentials. Start with the field notebook. I generally use a spiral-bound, five-inch by seven-inch memo book. Throw in several ball point pens and some pencils. Since several of the explorations will involve taking some measurements, a six-inch flexible ruler or tape measure is another essential. Include a small magnifier or hand lens. Nature centers generally stock good plastic lenses that cost less than three dollars. You could also get a battery-operated, hand-held, lighted magnifier (30x) moderately priced at about ten dollars. You may also want to have a bug box—a small see-through acrylic box with a magnifier permanently set into the lid. It's a handy item for examining such creatures as crab spiders, blister beetles, ants, and other small things. With it you can capture, hold, and study the creature without touching or harming it. Keep a pen knife in your kit as well. You'll use it for slicing into mushrooms, prying open seeds, and innumerable other tasks.

All the basic kit contents easily fit into a medium-sized Ziploc bag, ready to carry in the backpack, a bicycle basket, or the glove compartment of a car.

Basic Kit:
field notebook
ruler
magnifier
bug box
pen knife
pens and pencils
small sandwich bags

Although not essential, a pair of binoculars adds to the joy of discovery. Today there are many very good, inexpensive binoculars on the market. A camera is another useful tool for studying plants and animals.

For a few activities you'll need a bucket, glass jars with lids, a watch with a second hand, sticks, string, and a compass. You will also want a three-ringed loose-leaf notebook. Here you can enter, in an expanded form, the information collected in the field. As you make notes, you'll have an opportunity to reflect on what you saw and to think through some of the questions raised during your explorations. Consult your reference books and field guides for additional information.

You will understand as you read and investigate how fragile these communities of living things can be. You will inevitably encounter the effects of man's presence. I hope you will become concerned in specific, practical ways. This kind of concern is the way to make a difference for the future of the environment. We still have a long way to go.

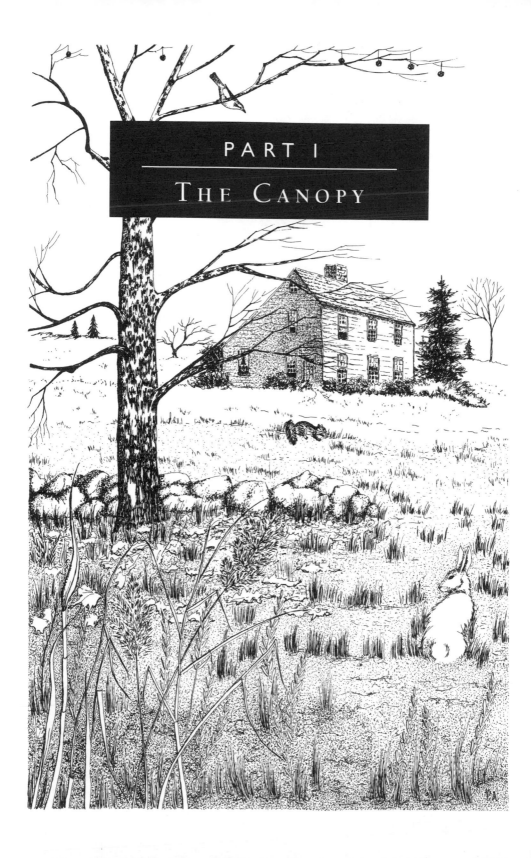

PART I

THE CANOPY

I N THE FOREST the topmost branches and leaves of the tallest trees create a living awning that protects the life below. If you take a walk in the woods on a summer day, you can feel the effects of this cover. The woodland is cool, shady, and damp because the trees cast a cooling shadow on the ground. The canopy protects small trees, shrubs, and other living things not only from the blazing summer sun but also from pelting rains, which can damage delicate plant life.

Plants release a great deal of water vapor as they grow. The canopy prevents this wetness from evaporating into the atmosphere. Because it remains within the forest system, the moisture can be used by woodland plants and soil creatures.

If you don't live in the forest, a tree-lined street can provide the same benefits. Neighborhood canopies are created by maples, box elders, oaks, and other species of tall trees. Sometimes trees have such dense canopies that there isn't enough light for grass, shrubs, or small trees to grow beneath them. This is also true in the forest.

The neighborhood canopy is home to a great many animals, insects, and birds. Most of these creatures move down from the trees to find food and return to care for their young, and to be safe from predators. On the following pages you will meet the trees that make up the canopy in your neighborhood, as well as some of the birds and animals that live there.

CHAPTER 1

Deciduous Trees

THE SILENT SENTINELS

Trees, standing strong and silent, are the largest of living things. Because they live such a long time and react to their environment, trees have valuable historical information hidden beneath the tough protective layers of bark. Through the patient efforts of researchers in dendrology (the study of trees), we now know about events that occurred as long ago as 6,000 B.C.

A well-known characteristic of trees is the pattern of concentric circles scribed in the inner wood. These ring patterns are most obvious and easily studied on the wood of deciduous trees—trees that shed their leaves each fall. You can easily see these concentric rings in the stump of a felled tree. These rings account for the exquisite wood-grain patterns found in fine furniture.

Leonardo da Vinci (1452–1519) first made the connection between the number of rings and the age of a tree, but the mechanism that produces the rings was not clearly understood until fairly recently. In 1901 Andrew Douglas began the first systematic analysis of tree rings. His extensive work in this area contributed a great deal to what is known today about tree growth.

A tree grows in length and in width. It grows in length both at the tips of the roots and in the buds at the tips of twigs and branches. In these places delicate developing tissue called meristem is found. When triggered by hormones, the meristem develops and causes the twigs and roots to grow longer.

Trees also grow in circumference. Cambium, the thin tissue responsible for this growth, lies beneath the bark. This tissue is only two or three cells thick. The cambium layer covers the entire tree, from the smallest rootlets to the most delicate branches. Through the action of the cambium, all parts of the tree become thicker.

How do both kinds of growth occur? Toward the end of winter, longer and longer periods of daylight trigger the manufacture of growth hormones, such as auxin and gibberellin, by embryonic tissue. This undeveloped tissue is located in the leaf buds at the ends of twigs and branches. The growth chemicals cause developing cells to grow and divide, adding length to the branches and height to the tree. At the root ends, similar events result in longer roots.

At about the same time, the growth hormones produced in the twigs and branches activate the girth-producing cambium. The cells of the cambium sheath grow vigorously toward the outside of the tree. After several weeks these cells mature and cease dividing. Stiffened with cellulose, these older cells become specialized into hollow, food-carrying tubes called phloem. The phloem system transports carbohydrates manufactured in the green leaves to the branches, trunk, and roots. As the phloem cells age, new cells replace them

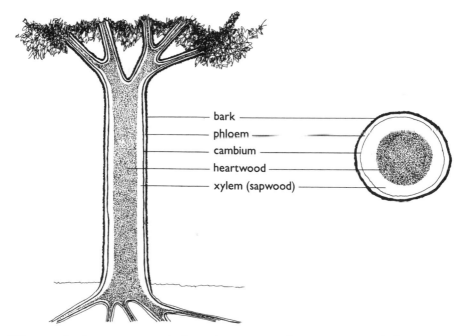

Phloem and xylem are composed of vascular structures that transport carbohydrates, water, and nutrients to nourish the tree.

and push them toward the outside of the tree. The old cells eventually become part of the outer bark. In a freshly cut log and with the help of a hand lens, you can sometimes see the living phloem as a circle of black dots just inside the outer bark.

The cambium produces another system of tubes that develop toward the inside of the tree. These tubes, called xylem, form microscopic pipelines that carry water and nutrients from the soil to the food-producing green leaves. In the spring, when hormonal activity is high, the newly formed xylem cells are large and have thin walls. This springwood or sapwood is the light component of an annual ring.

Later in the summer, growth hormones are no longer produced by the developing (meristematic) tissues. The cambium reacts to this lack of chemical activity by producing smaller cells with thick walls. These appear darker than the spring xylem cells and are called latewood. This cycle of xylem cell production is repeated every year. Together, the light bands of sapwood and the darker bands of latewood form the annual growth rings. In the fall, when growth slows, older xylem cells die and fill with lignin and other substances that produce rigidity in the tree. These xylem cells then become part of the nonliving heartwood of the tree. Dead wood makes up almost ninety-nine percent of the tree's volume.

In many deciduous trees the contrast between light and dark bands is not obvious. But in conifers (cone-bearing trees such as pine and spruce) the annual rings are distinct.

In the last twenty years the science of tree study has developed remarkably. Through a process called cross-dating, researchers can construct climatic maps to determine whether a climatic condition is normal for an area or is an aberration. Using the same technique scientists can construct models to study drought cycles and the effects of acid rain on tree growth. They're also discovering that the presence of trace metals, such as iron, aluminum, titanium, and copper, may help detect past and present surges in air pollution.

THE WORLD OF DECIDUOUS TREES

What to Bring
basic kit
protractor
graph paper
camera
file folder

Science Skills
observing
measuring
graphing

OBSERVATIONS

More than a thousand kinds of deciduous trees live in North America. The activities that follow will help you become better acquainted with deciduous trees and the way they work.

A good place to begin your tree study is in your backyard, a public park, or a golf course. Limit your search to a few trees at a time.

It is easier to identify a tree by examining its leaves than by examining its bark, flower, or shape, so begin your study when the trees are in leaf.

Trees and Their Leaves. The first step is to become familiar with the variety of leaf shapes and sizes. Pick a few obviously different trees. Are the leaves oval, heart-shaped, or elliptical? Are they lance-shaped or egg-shaped? Are they diamond or triangular?

Do any of the leaves have lobes? Are the edges serrated (toothlike), doubly serrated, or smooth? Are the edges wavy? You may find that one shape or edge pattern is more common.

How are the leaves arranged on the twig? Are they opposite each other or

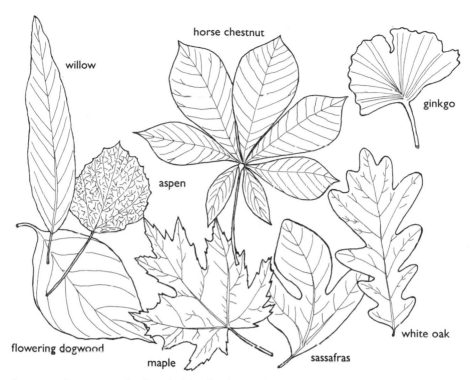

A tree can be most easily identified by the shape of its leaves. (Individual leaves are not drawn to scale.)

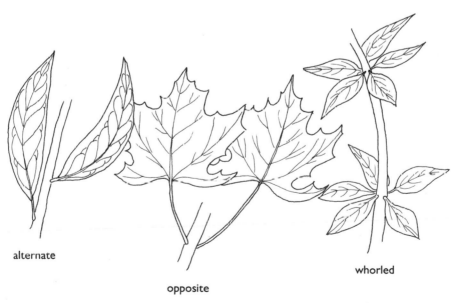

Leaves on a twig are arranged in one of three patterns.

are they alternately placed? Are they whorled, radiating out like spokes from a wagon wheel? Which is the most common leaf arrangement on the trees in your sample?

Are the leaves simple? Do they have one blade attached to the leaf stem? Or are they compound? Are there a few or several leaflets attached to the leaf stem?

Are the surfaces of the leaves smooth or rough? Are they hairy? Is the color or texture of the leaf the same or different on top and bottom surfaces?

Trees and Their Shapes. It is difficult to identify a tree based on its shape alone, but many trees do have characteristic shapes. To observe undistorted shapes, look for trees growing in open areas. The crowns of these trees will generally display the shape typical for that tree type better than those growing along crowded streets or in a grove.

Is the tree compact, with branches close to the main trunk, resulting in the oblong shape of a hickory? Is the crown wide and spreading like an oak's? Does it look like an upsidedown bud vase as does an elm? Do the branches grow out some distance from the main trunk and droop like a willow's?

Which Way Does the Wind Blow? Very often trees that grow in the open are bent in a particular direction. Prevailing summer winds affect the way they grow. Look at the trees in your area and see whether their crowns are bowing

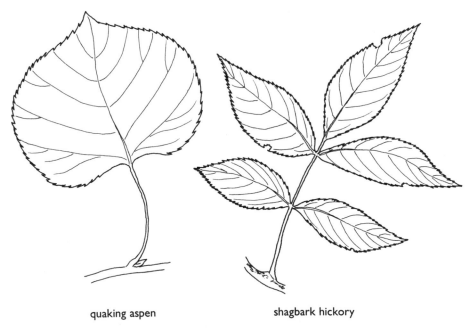

quaking aspen   shagbark hickory

A leaf may be simple (single) or compound (two or more leaflets).

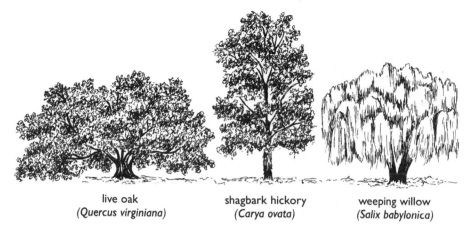

| live oak | shagbark hickory | weeping willow |
| (Quercus virginiana) | (Carya ovata) | (Salix babylonica) |

A mature tree growing in an open area can often be identified by its characteristic shape.

or nodding in the same way. Is this the direction of the prevailing winds during the summer?

The Autumn Extravaganza. During August many deciduous trees begin to put on their autumn colors. On what part of the tree do the yellows, oranges,

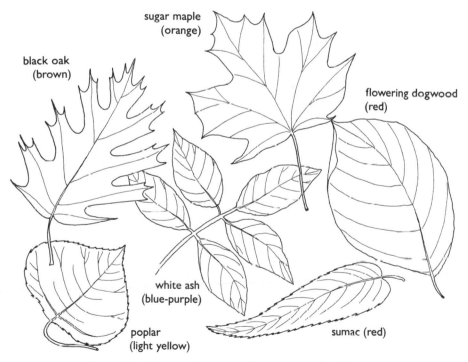

Be watching for nature's spectacular autumn color changes.

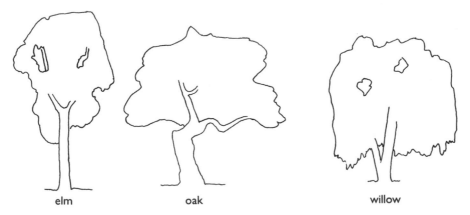

| elm | oak | willow |

Use these outlines to assist you in your mapping of some fall color changes.

or reds first appear: on the crown, or along one side? If on the side, is it the north, south, east, or west?

On the diagrams, you can map the pattern of color change as it appears on a few kinds of trees.

How long does it take one of your trees to change color? Is the time the same for other kinds of trees?

Is the pattern for color change the same for all trees of the same type? Is the progression of color change related to the part that receives shade or sunlight? Do different kinds of trees show a different pattern in the progression of color change? (See Chapter Note 1, on fall foliage.)

EXPLORATIONS

Broaden your survey of local trees to include more types. Make a tally sheet to display the number of times each type of tree appears in your survey. Use a field guide to help you identify the trees. If you can't find the name of a tree, make a drawing of its leaf.

TALLY SHEET OF NEIGHBORHOOD TREES

Tree Type	Number in Study Area
White Oak	
Sycamore	
Sweet Gum	
Catalpa	
Basswood	

The information on the talley sheet can be transferred to a histogram, which records not only the kinds of trees you have in the area but also the number of each kind of tree. A histogram is a tool used by field biologists to find the distribution of living things in a particular habitat.

Use the format shown in the following table to make a histogram of your own.

Show your histogram to some friends. Do a similar survey of the trees that grow in their neighborhoods. Compare the results. Try to explain some of the differences you find.

A Tree Portfolio. Make a tree portfolio. Take pictures of your trees

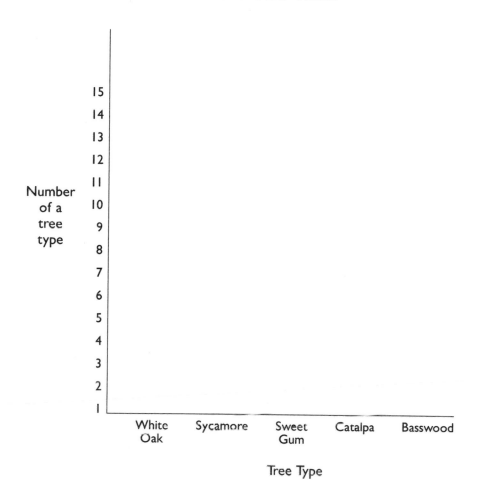

HISTOGRAM SHOWING FREQUENCY DISTRIBUTION OF NEIGHBORHOOD TREES

throughout the year. Your collection should include photographs of the trees' flowers, fruits, leaves, and bark. You may think that all bark looks alike, but you'll be surprised that you can identify a tree by the pattern of its bark.

Include the location of the tree and the date you took each picture in your portfolio.

How Tall Is That Tree? To measure the height of a standing tree all you need is a cardboard triangle, a measuring tape, and enough space around the tree to make your observations. This method of indirect measurement is based on the geometry of a right triangle that has two sides of equal length.

Make your triangle from a square piece of cardboard with sides of one foot. Cut the square from one corner to the opposite corner. This will give you two right triangles, but you will only need one of them to measure the height of your tree. The ground around the tree whose height you want to measure needs to be reasonably level for this method to work.

Walk away from the tree until you think you may be where the top of the tree would land if you cut it down. Face the tree. Hold the triangle so that one of the short sides is parallel to the ground and the other short side is parallel to the trunk of the tree. Now place the tip of the triangle that's closest to you at eye level. Pretend the long edge is a gunsight and you are shooting at the topmost twig. If you are too close to the tree, the sight will aim at a lower branch and you will have to walk backward until you see the tip of the tree in your "sight." If you are too far away, you will be aiming at the sky. In this case walk toward the tree until you see the top of the tree at the tip of the long side. When you are sighted just right (be sure to keep the bottom edge of the triangle parallel to the ground), you will be standing almost one tree height from the tree.

With your tape measure, measure the distance from the base of the tree to

shagbark hickory sycamore yellow birch

A tree may be identified from its distinctive bark. The outer covering of shagbark hickory is gray with long, loose scales. Sycamore has smooth, flat plates that slough off its trunk. The bark of yellow birch is smooth and peels in silver-yellow curly strips.

the spot where you are standing (A). Add to that your height from the ground to your eye (B). The sum of these two numbers will equal the approximate height of the tree, that is, $A + B = H$.

Is there a relationship between the height of the tree and the number of main branches on the tree? Using the same method as outlined above, find the height of several trees of the same species. Then count the main branches on each tree. It's easiest to count them if you stand under the tree and look up. You will need to find trees whose branches haven't been removed. Record the count for each tree.

Patterns in Branching. By the time winter arrives, deciduous trees have lost their leaves. The skeletons that remain are ideal for learning about branching patterns. Observe a few kinds of trees and describe their branching patterns.

Whorled branches grow out of the trunk in threes. It occurs rarely, but you can find it easily in pine trees.

The branches, twigs, and leaves are paired in some trees. Look for this pattern in maples, ashes, dogwoods, and horse chestnuts.

The third pattern of branch arrangement is called alternate. The branches and twigs grow in spiral steps. If you would like to learn more about patterns in nature, read Trudi Hammel Garland's book, *Fascinating Fibonaccis*, as listed in the bibliography.

Observe a tree from a distance. Are the branches growing in any particular direction? Besides the prevailing winds, what might cause the tree to grow more on one side than the other, or to lean in one direction?

A Twig Collection. Twigs come in a variety of sizes, shapes, colors, and textures. Make a collection of twigs, starting with beech, oak, hickory, and maple, if you can find them. How many colors did you find among your twigs? Were the twigs straight, zigzag, or curved? Use the outline below to study additional twig traits.

Terminal bud: Is it large? Sticky? Pointed? Rounded or cigar-shaped? Is it smooth or hairy? Watch the tree through the spring and find out what develops from this end bud. (See Chapter Note 2, on buds.)

Side buds: How do they resemble the terminal bud?

Lenticels: Are they present on each of your twigs? Is there any pattern to their arrangement? How far back from the tip of the twig can you find them? (See Chapter Note 3, on lenticels.)

Leaf scar: Compare the leaf scars on each of your twigs. (See Chapter Note 4, on leaf scars.)

Terminal bud scale scar: This is the point where the bud scales of the

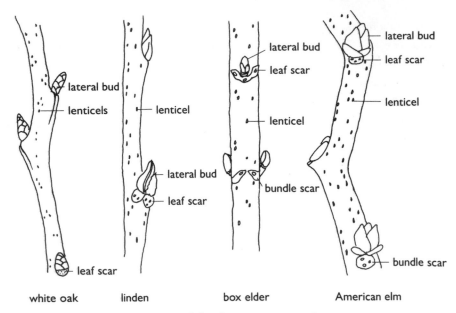

Different species exhibit characteristic growth patterns.

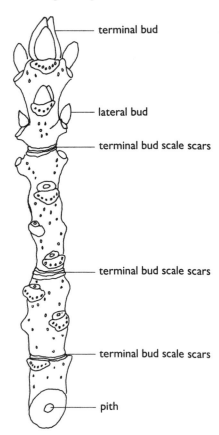

The annual growth of this green ash twig can be determined by measuring the distance between successive terminal bud scale scars.

THE CANOPY

terminal bud were attached. The distance between each ring, which looks like a rubber band around the twig, is equal to one year's growth. In what year did your twig grow the most? Look at other twigs the same age on the same tree. Did they also grow the most in that year?

Pith: In each type of tree, twigs show a pattern of pith unique to the tree type. Cut a cross section of twig and examine the pith. If it is star-shaped, it is probably an oak, poplar, or hickory twig. If the pith is circular, you probably have a twig from an elm. (See Chapter Note 5, on pith.)

Make a chart that will show similarities and differences between the twigs from different trees.

CHAPTER NOTES

1. **Fall Foliage.** The green pigment chlorophyll is essential for the plants to convert water, carbon dioxide, and light energy into carbohydrates. This process is called photosynthesis. Oxygen, a by-product of the process, is released.

As summer progresses, the days get shorter. In response, deciduous trees remove food from their leaves. This causes the chlorophyll to disintegrate.

In addition to the green chlorophylls, other pigments called carotenoids are present, but in smaller quantities. The carotenoids include yellow carotenes and pale yellow xanthophylls. Another leaf pigment is anthocyanin. This pigment responds to the acidity of the sap in the leaf. If the sap is acidic or has high levels of sugar, anthocyanins will show brilliant red in the foliage. When the sap is less acidic, the leaves appear a bluish purple. Red and yellow pigments sometimes blend to produce orange.

2. **Buds.** The developing tissue in the terminal bud adds length to the twig. The lateral buds, those that grow along the side of the twig, produce flowers, leaves, or new branches.

3. **Lenticels.** The small dots you see on the new or young twigs are lenticels. These are openings in the outer layers of the stem and root tissues that allow the exchange of oxygen into, and carbon dioxide out of, the plant.

4. **Leaf Scars.** During the summer the tree produces a layer of cork between the leaf stem and the point where it attaches to the twig. When this layer is complete the leaf falls and the mark on the twig is called the leaf scar. The shape of the leaf scar is unique for each type of tree. If you look closely at a bare twig, you will see tiny dots in the leaf scar. Each of these dots represents the place where the transport tubes of the twig joined those of the leaf. The dots are called the vascular bundle scar.

5. **Pith.** If you cut into a twig, you will find a spongelike substance called pith. When placed in a growth medium, pieces of pith grow into new plants.

CHAPTER 2

The Pine Family

A LIFE-STYLE UNDER SIEGE

In October 1987 there was an exceptionally early snowfall in New England. The storm occurred when most deciduous trees like oaks and maples were still carrying their leaves. These trees could not support the weight of the falling snow and ice. Branches, even large ones, broke off. The storm destroyed as much as ten percent of the hardwoods.

In contrast, coniferous evergreens growing in the same area showed no damage from the freezing snow and killing winds. The evergreens escaped harm because of some vital adaptations made for life in the snowy north.

The leaves of coniferous evergreens, usually called needles, remain green throughout the year. During the winter months each needle continues to be a solar-powered food factory, manufacturing carbohydrates from carbon dioxide and water. Because the needles remain on the tree year-round, they must shed snow readily. The broad, flat, deciduous leaf does not.

Although many coniferous evergreens don't shed their needles in the autumn, the needles are not a permanent part of the tree. They grow old, turn brown, fall, and are replaced by new growth. Since only a small percentage of the needles fall at one time, the tree is never bare. The life span of eastern white pine (*Pinus strobus*) needles is only two to three years, whereas the leaves of the spruces (*Picea* sp.) remain on the tree up to six years. Native to the high elevations of California is the bristlecone pine (*Pinus aristata*), which keeps its leaves for as long as twenty-five to thirty years. Often its branches have so many needles that each resembles a large foxtail. Longevity of needles, however, doesn't necessarily indicate productivity. Scientists have discovered that each year an evergreen needle becomes forty percent less efficient in food production.

Conifers have developed several strategies for survival. Feel a needle: It's slender and tough, and it has a waxy coat. These features help the trees endure the rigors of the winter months. During this harsh period, the greatest threat to evergreens is the winter drought, as water is unavailable to the tree when frozen. The needle's small surface area and waxy coat prevent water from escaping from the leaf.

Another adaptation of conifers allows them to live in austere habitats and flourish in impoverished soils. Mineral particles suspended in air currents are trapped and held by the needles. A rain or snow storm then washes the minerals from the leaves and they enter the soil directly beneath the tree. There the tree's root system absorbs them. This ability to extract even minimal amounts of mineral nourishment from both the atmosphere and nutrient-poor soil gives conifers an advantage in inhospitable environments.

The water-conserving needles of the white spruce (Picea glauca) *help it survive in its dry mountain habitat.*

In addition to water and nutrients, evergreens need sunlight. If you could look down on the branches from above, you would see that the needles are arranged so that each gets maximum exposure to the sun. No single needle is ever in the shadow of another for very long.

Evergreens' conical shape is an advantage, too. What better way to shed the weight of heavy, wet snow than to have it slide effortlessly down the sides? The branches even have an elastic quality that helps them spring back into place without damage.

Both deciduous trees and conifers have strategies for surviving insect attacks. Before their leaves are completely eaten, some deciduous trees may shed their damaged leaves and grow new ones.

Some evergreens and many deciduous trees handle the insect problems by producing toxic chemicals that keep some insect populations away, thus protecting their leaves. Unfortunately, spruce trees do not have such defenses

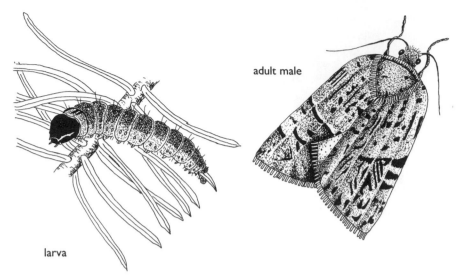

adult male

larva

The spruce budworm (Choristoneura fumiferana) *feeds on spruce needles.*

against the spruce budworm, a serious pest of eastern forests. The caterpillars that emerge from cocoons in the spring do extensive damage.

All these adaptations help conifers meet the challenges of snow, drought, freezing temperatures, short days, rocky soil, and insects. These trees are designed for living on the edge. They aren't so well suited for the stresses of our high-tech society, however. The very maneuvers that these ancient species use to extract moisture and minerals from the air make them highly susceptible to atmospheric pollutants. Acid rain is destroying our coniferous forests at an alarming rate.

Larches, of the genus *Larix*, are also members of the pine group but, unlike the rest of that family, shed their needles each fall.

THE WORLD OF THE PINE FAMILY

What to Bring
basic kit
thermometer
camera
binoculars

Science Skills
observing
comparing

OBSERVATIONS

The pine family is a very large group of conifers. Most of its members are familiar Christmas tree species. The pine family includes larches or tamaracks

(*Larix* sp.), spruces (*Picea* sp.), hemlocks (*Tsuga* sp.), Douglas-firs (*Pseudotsuga* sp.) and, of course, pines (*Pinus* sp.).

In the activities that follow you will have a chance to look at many of these marvelous trees. Winter is a good time to begin making observations, when pines stand out among the skeletons of deciduous trees.

Variations in the Pine Family. Find a few different members of the pine family. What is the shape of each? Is it triangular? Does the tree look stiff and rigid or does it have a light, feathery look? How do the colors compare? Are they blue-green, yellow-green, or some other shade?

Look at the needles on the twigs. How are they arranged? In little bundles? How many needles are in each bundle? Is there a tan wrap around the base of each bundle? Roll one of the needles between your fingers. Is it round or angular? Cut across the needle and, with a hand lens, look at its shape.

In some members of the pine family, such a spruce and hemlock, the needles grow singly on the twigs, rather than in bundles. Are the needles attached to the twigs by little stems?

Look for cones. Where on the tree do you find them? At the top third of the tree? The top half? At the ends of the twigs?

A Conifer Game. Select one of your trees and write a description of it. Give your description and the tree's general location to a friend. Can your friend find it without further help from you? What was most helpful in your description? Least helpful?

Key Traits of Pine Family Members. Each of the many types of evergreens

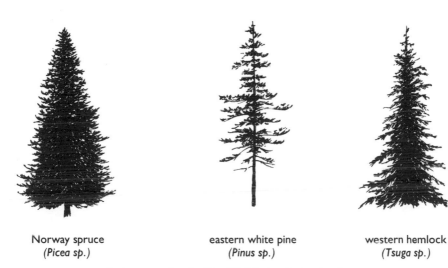

Norway spruce
(*Picea* sp.)

eastern white pine
(*Pinus* sp.)

western hemlock
(*Tsuga* sp.)

A pine can often be identified by its distinctive shape.

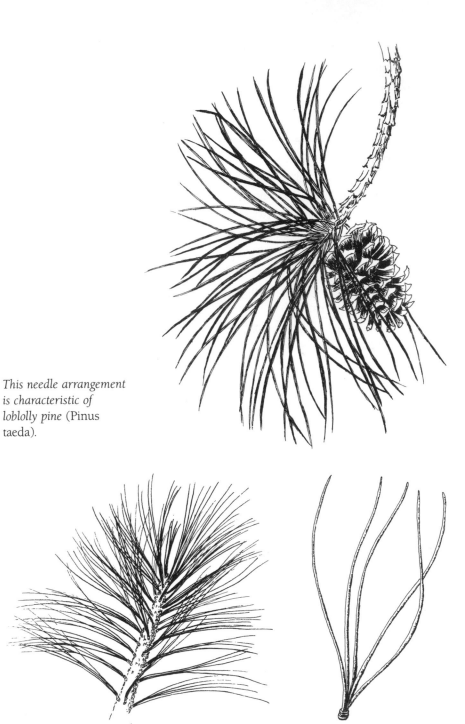

This needle arrangement is characteristic of loblolly pine (Pinus taeda).

The soft, bluish green needles of the eastern white pine (Pinus strobus) are three to five inches long and grow in bundles of five held together by a tan wrap, or sheath.

has special characteristics that distinguish it from the others. Several groups of pines are found throughout North America.

To which groups do your trees belong?

Pine (*Pinus*): The only cone-bearing evergreens that actually have needle-shaped leaves.

Make a cross section of a pine needle and examine the cut with a magnifier. If the needle is from a soft pine, you will see only one vein. If it is from a hard pine, you will see two veins.

Spruce (*Picea*): The shape of the tree is pyramidlike. The needles have sharp points, grow separately on the twig, and stick out in all directions so the twig does not lie flat. Needles are four-sided, grow on short pegs, and leave rough spots where they have fallen off.

Hemlock (*Tsuga*): This tree has a feathery appearance and characteristic nodding topknot. The needles of the eastern hemlock are dark green and flat. They grow in one plane, so the twigs lie flat. Look for white lines on the undersurface of the needles. These are caused by closely packed breathing pores or stomates.

True Fir (*Abies*): The bark is smooth with resin blisters. Needles occur singly, if you remove one, you will see a round scar. The needles tend to curve upward and look as though they grow out of the top of twig. Cones sit upright

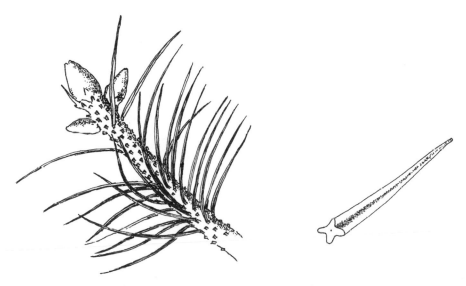

The four-sided needles of spruce (Picea sp.) grow singly on short projections, or pegs. When the needles fall off the twig, these pegs make the twig rough to the touch. In enlarged cross section, the four-sided design of an individual needle is apparent.

on the branches and don't fall in one piece like those of other conifers. The scales with their seeds fall individually from the cones.

Larch *(Larix)*: This pyramid-shaped tree is the only member of the pine family that sheds its needles each fall after turning a spectacular yellow-orange. The soft needles are apple-green and grow in tufts on stubby twigs. Look for knobs that cover twigs and branches.

Douglas-Fir *(Pseudotsuga)*: This member of the family is found only west of the Rocky Mountains. Cones are found on upper and lower branches. A three-pronged bract protrudes from behind every scale.

Barks in the Pine Family. When people draw trees, they almost always color the bark brown. How accurate is this common perception?

To improve your color observations, go to the paint section of a hardware store and select some color samples you think might match the trunks of cone-bearing trees. Include browns, tans, rusts, grays, and black.

With paint chips and notebook in hand, visit some evergreens and compare the colors with the tree trunks. Record your observations by cutting the matching colors from the paint charts and securing them in your notebook, along with other information about the tree.

Photograph the bark at different times of day to record how shifting angles of sunlight affect color. Caption each photograph with the name of the species, its location, the date and time, the side of the trunk you photographed (north, south, east, or west), and the approximate age of the tree. (See below for a method of estimating tree age.)

Examine some twigs. Is the bark at the tip of the twig the same as the bark farther back? Look at the bark on a branch. How does it differ from the bark of the twig? (See Chapter Note 1, on growth.)

Evergreens can be identified by the patterns of plates, cracks, ridges, and fissures in the bark. The size and shape of plates in the bark change as the tree ages and expands its girth. Examine the bark on the trunks of your trees. Are the cracks vertical or horizontal? Are they slanted? How wide are they? What size and shape are the plates?

Examine the bark on younger evergreens and compare it with the bark of older trees?

Cradles of the Pines. When we talk of evergreen cones, we are usually talking about the more conspicuous female, or seed-bearing, cones. (See Chapter 3 for male cones.) These cones are as varied as the trees that produce them. Carefully examine cones from different trees. Are they soft and pliable or hard and rigid? How long are they? How wide? Do they have prickles?

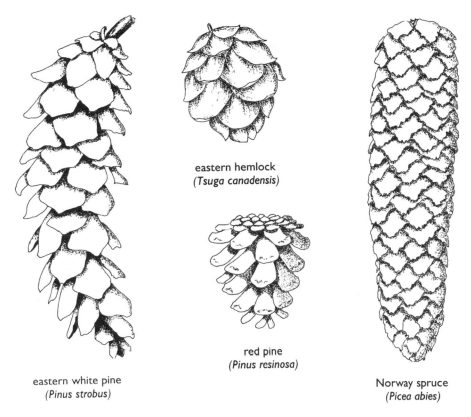

eastern hemlock
(*Tsuga canadensis*)

red pine
(*Pinus resinosa*)

eastern white pine
(*Pinus strobus*)

Norway spruce
(*Picea abies*)

Cones are the seed-bearing structures that have evolved to ensure the propagation of the pines.

How are the cones attached to the twig? Is there a stalk? Are the cones growing opposite each other on the twig? Are the cones curved or straight?

Examine a few scales from a cone. Do you see scars or slight depressions in the scales? How many depressions are there on each scale? Are there any seeds in your cones? (See Chapter Note 2, on number of seeds.)

EXPLORATIONS

The Pines As Windbreaks. The members of the pine family make excellent windbreaks. You can discover this for yourself on any cold and windy winter day. Visit a dense grove of conifers, standing on all sides of the trees. What differences did you notice? Did you notice any difference in the sound of the wind?

Do groves of evergreens have any effect on temperature? Record the temperatures on the different sides and compare.

Christmas Treasures. With the arrival of Christmas, you will have a wonderful opportunity to explore further the world of evergreens. Visit a tree market and ask permission to forage for pieces of trunk, discarded branches, and twigs.

Which evergreen species is most commonly sold for Christmas trees? Ask the salesperson whether buyers prefer one type of evergreen. Where were the trees grown? When were they cut?

Inspect the branches on one tree. Is the bark at the tip the same as in the middle of the branch? Examine the trunk. Is the bark at the top the same as it is at the base?

Find a tree that is lying down. How are the branches arranged on the trunk? Are they opposite each other? Are they alternately placed, as in a series of steps? Do three or more branches grow from the same level on the trunk, like spokes of a wagon wheel? Is this growth pattern the same for the twigs?

Age of the Tree. Since a whorl of branches forms on the tree each year, you can find out how old pines and spruces are by counting the number of whorls. Don't forget to count the whorls made by branches that have been removed. The evidence for these branches will be scars on the trunk. What is the age of the youngest Christmas tree? The oldest? What's the average age?

Survey some living trees. What is the average age of trees of one species in your neighborhood? What age is the oldest tree of this species? The youngest? How can you find out what the life span of that species is?

Another method used to determine the age of a tree is counting the rings in a piece of trunk. Cut segments of trunk from a tree that has been thrown away after the holidays. Get disks from the lower and upper portions of the trunk. Lightly sand these disks to see the rings better. (See Chapter 1 for information about growth rings.)

Using a disk from the lower trunk, determine the age of the tree. Compare the number of rings at the base of the tree with that at the top.

Measure the width of each ring to determine how much the tree grew each year. Is this the same for both disks?

The Evergreen As a Host. Some mushrooms have developed mutually beneficial relationships with many species of evergreens. Below the ground, these mushrooms produce a network of threads called hyphae. When the hyphae touch young tree roots, they enfold the rootlets in a sheath. Some hyphae penetrate the roots, creating a mycorrhiza, or "fungus-root." This arrangement provides food for the fungus and greatly increases the area from which the root can absorb water and minerals.

Other kinds of relationships are not so helpful for the trees. Beetle larvae

The wagon-wheel branch arrangement of the Norway spruce (Picea abies) *is typical of pine family members.*

hatch from eggs and feed on the soft tissue of inner bark, etching deep grooves called galleries. The galleries can be seen after the outer bark falls off. Some grooves are randomly scribed in the bark; others are herringbone. Foresters can identify the species of beetle by gallery patterns.

Harmful bracket fungi grow inside damaged or dying evergreens. The familiar shelf or bracket on the outside of the tree is the fruiting body of the fungi. It manufactures spores. These windblown spores gain entrance to other trees through existing wounds, woodpecker holes, or unhealed fire damage.

CHAPTER NOTES

1. **Tree Growth.** Conifers grow during the warm season and rest when the weather turns cold. By midsummer, growth for that year is complete and you can find terminal buds on the twigs. Within these buds are immature

structures that will develop into next season's needles, pollen cones, and seed cones. At the beginning of the next growing season, the cells elongate and develop.

2. Number of Seeds. To find the number of seeds in a cone, count the number of scales. Multiply that number by two, since each scale carries two seeds. Use a pair of binoculars to count the number of female cones on the top portion of the tree. Multiply that number by the number of seeds per cone to get an approximate number of seeds produced by that tree.

CHAPTER 3

Seeds

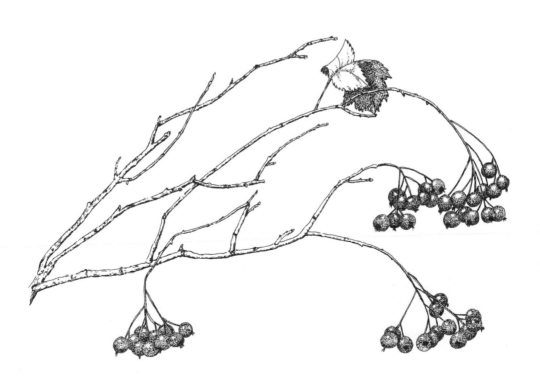

THE CRADLES OF LIFE

Autumn is harvest time for people living in the northern hemisphere. It is also harvest time for small mammals, many birds, and even some insects. In September and October, when seeds become mature, squirrels and chipmunks begin to hoard grains and nuts. By November, blue jays, grosbeaks, chicka-dees, and titmice are feeding on sunflower, thistle, and millet seeds. Through-out the winter, deer mice and other small mammals search for life-sustaining seeds.

Seeds are a valuable winter food source because they contain a high level of nutrients. Seeds are rich in nitrogen and essential amino acids, which are the building blocks of animal protein. Seeds also contain sugars and fats— sources of energy that can be stored in the animal body for use during the cold months that lie ahead.

When metabolized, fat provides more energy than could be produced by an equal weight of carbohydrate. Birds and seed-eating mammals need to eat foods that will give them the most energy for the least effort. Seeds, with their high fat content, can do that.

Seeds are the relatively new invention of a large group of highly specialized plants. Seed-bearing plants first appeared during the Triassic period some two hundred million years ago. The earliest seed plants were the gymnosperms, ancestors of our present-day pines, spruces, and firs. Gymnosperm comes from a Greek word meaning "naked seed." This refers to the fact that seeds of cone-bearing plants develop on the scales of the cones and not within the protective wall of a plant ovary.

Cones provide an important service for the coniferous tree. The cones carry the seeds, which themselves carry the embryo with its genes that are the blueprints needed to build the next generation of trees.

Cones come in two versions: male and female. The pollen-producing male cones grow in clusters on the lower branches; the larger female cones develop in the upper branches. On any given tree the male and female cones do not mature at the same time. This strategy sidesteps the genetic problems that often develop when closely related individuals interbreed.

When the male cones first appear early in the spring, they are closed tightly. Later the mature cones open and release enormous amounts of pollen, which contains male sex cells. Shaking a branch of pollen-laden cones will produce a yellow cloud of pollen dust. Each type of tree produces pollen grains that differ in shape, size, and texture from those produced by other trees. These characteristics of pollen grains have been used to identify tree species.

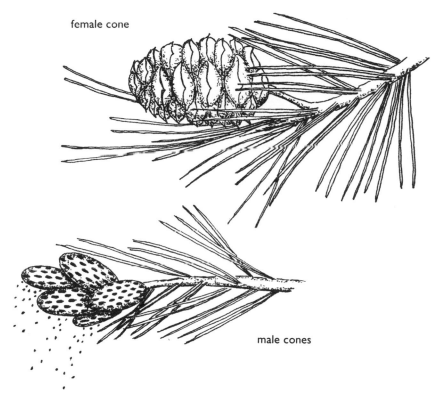

female cone

male cones

Seeds contained in the female cone are fertilized by pollen-bearing male cones.

Paleontologists have found pollen grain fossils that help them reconstruct the evolutionary history of gymnosperms.

How does pollen find a female cone from its own species? Each species produces female cones that are cleverly designed "wind traps." As air currents pass over a cone, the subsequent air-flow patterns will guide only the proper pollen inside the cone to the egg structures. Factors such as the shape of the cone, its length and diameter, the number of scales, and the speed of the wind determine these patterns.

Pines have two additional tricks for trapping pollen and further ensuring seed production. The female cone is surrounded by needles. As the pollen-laden wind passes through the spaces between the needles, its speed decreases. The pollen grains suspended in the air are thus dumped on the downwind side of the needle windbreak and onto the cone.

If you watch the branches of pines as the wind blows through them, you will notice another trick for trapping pollen. The branches are set so that the wind spirals down through them. The cones can then sweep from a larger volume of surrounding air.

Only one in every several thousand grains of pollen ever pollinates a female cone. The rest are left to collide with bushes, trees, raindrops, people, and anything else in their way. This may seem like a risky scheme for reproducing, but the long history of cone-bearing plants proves that the method works.

After the female cones are pollinated, winged seeds are produced. These seeds develop on the inside of the bracts of the female cones. Seeds mature in a two-and-one-half-year cycle but the cones of some species, such as pitch pine and jack pine, remain closed for several years.

About fifty million years after the appearance of coniferous trees, angiosperms, or flowering plants, made their debut on the evolutionary stage. Angiosperm is an umbrella term that covers a wide range of plant types, from the prized cultivars in your garden to the unadorned weeds along the roadside.

Although we don't think of trees such as oaks, maples, and willows as flowering plants, they are. In the spring their tiny, inconspicuous flowers produce lightweight pollen that is carried aloft by the spring breezes. Other deciduous trees, such as flowering dogwood, hawthorn, and black locust produce sweet-smelling flowers that lure insects to do the pollinating for them.

Angiosperm seeds develop within the walls of ovaries. Mature seeds are wrapped in the protective remnants of the ovary, such as the oak's acorn, the "itchy ball" of the sycamore, and the winged samara of the maple.

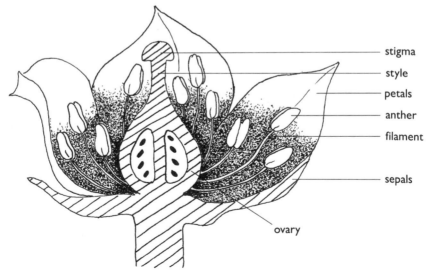

The seeds of an angiosperm mature within a closed ovary.

These seed containers look and feel different from apples and peaches, but they are also called fruits because they developed from the same flower structures, the ovaries.

As you begin to look at different trees, you will find that not all trees produce their fruits at the same time. Some trees' fruits are ripe by early summer while others don't mature until fall.

THE WORLD OF SEEDS

What to Bring
basic kit
binoculars
camera

Science Skills
observing
measuring

OBSERVATIONS

The Cones and Seeds of the Pine Family. Wherever you live you can usually find members of the pine family. Look for spruce, fir, hemlock, and of course pines.

Pines: Male Cones. In the early spring look for the small pollen-producing cones growing on the lower branches of a pine tree. What color are the cones? How do they feel? Do they crumble easily? How big are they? Are they in bunches or are they arranged singly on the branches? Are the cones shielded by needles or are they exposed? Observe them throughout the spring. What changes occur in the cones as they mature?

Pines: Female Cones. Look for these cones on the upper branches of the same tree. You may need binoculars to get a good look at them. How are the cones arranged on the tree? Are they side by side? Do the tips of the cone point toward the trunk or away? Are they grouped in bunches? Do the cones hang from the branch by a stem or are they attached directly?

These cones are often out of reach, so you will have to rely on those you find beneath the tree for a closer look. Are they brown, reddish brown, gray-brown, or some other color? Are the scales of the cones open or closed? Look for cones with at least some of the scales closed.

A green cone with tightly closed scales is probably immature. The seeds inside are similarly immature, but it's worth a look to discover for yourself. You may find mature cones lying on the ground that are still closed. Take one indoors and wait a day or two for the scales to open. If the cone does not open, you can try to coax it by putting it on a warm radiator or dipping it briefly into boiling water. Then you can get a good look at the winged seeds of a conifer and how they are arranged within the cone. How many seeds are there on each scale? Look for the seed scar on the scale. Each winged seed is covered by a hard, protective coat. What advantage is this for the seed?

A Collection of Cones. Now that you've examined the male and female cones from one kind of evergreen, you can look for male and female cones on other kinds of conifers. Observe the cones throughout a growing season. How do the male and female cones of one tree differ from those of others? (See Chapter Note for clues.) Use the chart below to help you organize your discoveries.

Find the seeds within closed cones. Compare the seeds from different members of the pine family. How many grow on each scale? Do they all have wings?

Collect cones from the trees or photograph them instead. Record such info as:

CONES

Photograph	Description	Location on the Tree
spruce	Soft and squeezable Two seeds per scale No prickles	
pines, soft		
pines, hard		
hemlock		
true fir		
Douglas-fir		

The Fruits and Seeds of Angiosperms. Oaks, maples, ashes, willow, hickories, catalpa, sycamore, and fruit trees such as cherry, apple, and pear, are angiosperms. This means that their seeds are found inside a ripened ovary, or fruit, such as the pod from a catalpa tree or the acorn from an oak.

The fruits of angiosperms are categorized as either fleshy or dry. Fleshy fruits have soft, fleshlike tissue under the outside skin. Some examples of fleshy fruits are apples, peaches, and mulberries. Look for the trees in your neighborhood that have fleshy fruits.

Dry fruits have a dry, generally hard tissue beneath the outer coat. There are two groups of dry fruits. In one, the mature fruits can be split apart. Look

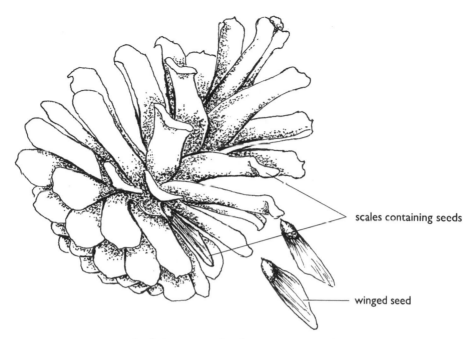

scales containing seeds

winged seed

Seeds in an open female cone rest on scales.

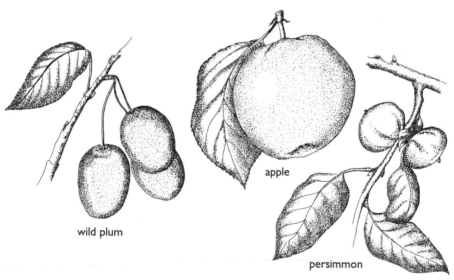

apple

wild plum

persimmon

Trees may produce fleshy fruits as part of their reproductive strategy. The edible fruit of the wild plum (a drupe) is found between the hard and bony inner ovary wall and the soft and fleshy outer wall. The outer ovary wall, or skin, of an apple (a pome) is fleshy and the inner ovary wall, or core, is like cartilage. The seeds of persimmon are distributed throughout the fleshy fruit of this berry.

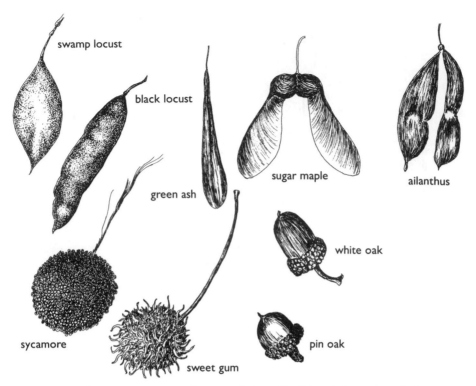

Dry fruits come in many shapes and sizes. (Fruit is not drawn to scale.)

for trees, such as black locust, that produce this kind of fruit. A field guide will help you in your search.

In the second group of dry fruits, the mature fruits cannot be split easily. The fruits of this group are samaras, achenes, and nuts.

Samaras. The samaras, or winged seeds, of all maple trees develop in pairs. Each member of the pair contains a maple seed. In the spring, look for samaras of silver maple, Norway maple, box elder, red maple, mountain maple, and striped maple. Keep a record of your observations. Include a tracing of a samara from each of the different trees. How are the samaras alike and how are they different?

Samaras that develop on ashes, elms, yellow poplars, ailanthus, and bass-wood do not grow in pairs. Find some of these samaras and compare them with each other and with those from the maples.

On which kinds of trees do the samaras grow in clusters? What is the largest number of winged seeds you can find in a cluster? Which trees retain their samaras during the winter months? What advantage is it for the tree to hold its seeds until the spring?

Achenes. These are the fuzzy seeds found on the "itchy balls" of sycamores. Not all "itchy balls" fall from the tree during the autumn. You can see many of them dangling from sycamore branches throughout the winter.

Nuts. Another group of dry fruits that don't split at maturity is the nuts. The well-known acorns of oak trees belong to this group. Hickories, walnuts, pecans, and chestnuts are other examples of nuts.

EXPLORATIONS

How Many Seeds? Seed plants produce a huge number of seeds each year. The number of seeds produced greatly exceeds the number that will find suitable conditions to germinate and develop into new plants. How many is a huge number?

Find a samara-producing tree. You will probably want to select a small tree for this activity.

1. Count the number of seeds per samara.
2. Count the number of samaras on a branch. (For our purposes, a branch is a large, secondary stem growing from the main trunk.)
3. Count the branches on your tree.
4. How many samaras are on the tree?
5. How many seeds are on the tree?
6. How many of this kind of tree are there in your neighborhood?
7. How many seeds (potential trees) of this type could be in your neighborhood?

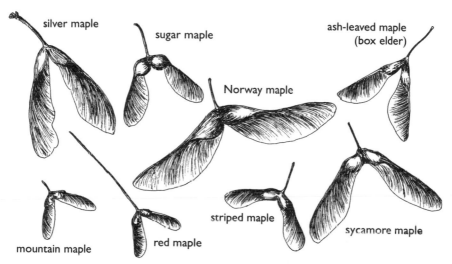

There is some variety in the appearance of samaras of different species of maple, but the basic design is the same. Each consists of a pair of winged seeds.

How Do Samaras Work? Watch the way samaras spin downward through the air. Samaras from different kinds of trees fall in different ways. Collect samaras from different kinds of trees. Samaras from sugar maples aren't available until fall, but silver maple samaras can be found in the spring.

To find out how they fall you could simply throw them into the air and watch them return to the ground. For a better look, throw them from a ladder or a second-story window. Are they rollers, tumblers, or undulators? You might like a friend to help you observe your falling samaras.

Do the fruits of ash, maple, ailanthus, and yellow poplar all fall in the same way? Group them as to whether they roll, tumble, or undulate.

Measure the length and width of samaras from different trees. Does size influence the way it falls?

Remove the wings from some samaras in your collection and drop them from the same height as the winged samaras. How do the wings affect the fall of the fruit?

How does a breeze affect the fall of a samara? What advantage is a samara to the tree species?

CHAPTER NOTE

Clues to Distinguish Cones. Cones and seeds from various members of the pine family have recognizable differences.

Hemlocks have small (half-inch), globular, conelike flowers on the developing female cones at the tips of twigs. The male cones are small and can be found among the needles a short distance from the tips. The female cones mature and produce seeds in one season.

The male cones of spruces grow along the sides of the branches. They wither and disappear after the pollen grains disperse. The larger female cones develop at the tips of branches in the top third of the tree.

Male and female cones of firs develop in essentially the same areas of the twigs as do the cones of other conifers. The male cones develop on the underside of the branches. The female cones develop on the upper side and mature in one year. They disintegrate and leave behind an upright telltale spike.

CHAPTER 4

Gray Squirrels

CIVILIZED ACROBATS

Many wild mammals share our urban and suburban neighborhoods. Gray squirrels are among the few that take no precautions to hide from us. In fact, they seem to delight in showing off, leaping gracefully from tree to tree or racing headlong down a tree trunk.

Gray squirrels belong to an order of mammals called rodents. The order contains beavers, chipmunks, and voles, as well as the less popular rats and mice.

The squirrel family includes the burrowing ground squirrels, such as prairie dogs, thirteen-lined ground squirrels, arctic ground squirrels, eastern chipmunks, and groundhogs (woodchucks), as well as the flying squirrels and the tree squirrels.

Members of the tree squirrel group are the eastern gray squirrel (*Sciurus carolinensis*), the western gray squirrel (*S. griseus*), the eastern fox squirrel (*S. niger*), and the red squirrel (*S. hudsonian*), sometimes called the spruce squirrel.

Human beings have removed much of the squirrel's natural habitat to make way for housing, roads, and shopping malls. Many gray squirrels can no longer depend on seeds and nuts once provided by beech, oak, and hickory forests, so they have had to learn new ways to get food. Squirrels have skillfully cracked the codes of our "squirrel-proof" bird feeders to get to the nutritious seeds. Urbanized gray squirrels have even learned how to beg a snack from visitors in public parks. With these new sources of food, an urban acre can accommodate as many as twenty squirrels.

The gray squirrels in the hardwood forests tell a different story. They have to work for their meals and competition is keen. One squirrel per acre is the rule of thumb here.

Since there is a greater variety of trees and shrubs in most wooded areas, woodland squirrels have a more varied diet than their urban cousins, but it is determined by seasonal trends. In the spring gray forest squirrels dine on the tiny, delicate flowers of oaks and other nut trees. As spring gives way to summer, the fruits of red mulberry, apple, and black cherry trees are their preferred foods. Squirrels will also feed on less desirable foods, such as mushrooms, grass, leaves, insects, and small birds.

Like all rodents, squirrels come with two pairs of curved, chisel-shaped incisor teeth, ideal for gnawing nutshells and tree bark. Unlike our teeth, the squirrel's grow throughout its life at a rate of about five or six inches each year. To prevent its teeth from growing awkwardly large, the squirrel instinctively grinds its teeth on almost anything hard—tree bark, animal bones, the hard

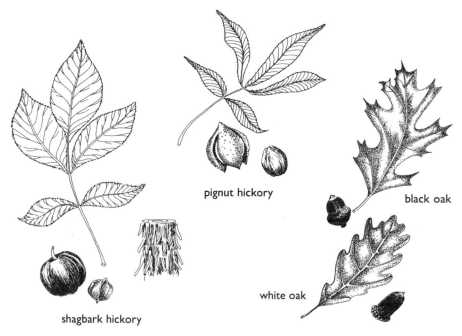

Squirrels display a preference for the dry fruit of specific trees.

shells of nuts. Not all objects are as safe as hickory nuts. Some squirrels have had an enlightening experience with electrical wires.

Squirrels quickly learn the most efficient way to open each kind of nut. With four fingers and a stubby thumb on each front paw, they can spin and flip a nut with amazing dexterity.

Squirrels have favorite foods, usually nuts that are high in energy and easy to open. Since hickory nuts have twice the calories of acorns, it's no surprise that these nuts are favorites. Nuts from shagbark hickories are the best of all. Thin-shelled pignuts are easy to open, but they are not economical food for squirrels because the edible part is small.

When hickories are not available, squirrels often forage around white oaks looking for the sweet-tasting acorns. Acorns from black oaks are bitter, so squirrels avoid them.

Squirrels bury a great many nuts each fall, but they don't always remember where they stashed them. They retrieve many of the nuts they bury through their excellent sense of smell. The remaining nuts often germinate, becoming black walnut, butternut, beechnut, oak, and hickory trees. Squirrels thus plant many trees throughout our parks and forests.

Gray squirrel reproduction is directly proportional to the number of nuts produced on each squirrel's home range. When nut productivity is low, squirrel birthrate is correspondingly low. One reason for a small nut crop could be a late spring frost. Freezing temperatures at this time often destroy developing flowers on oak, hickory, and other nut trees. Fewer flowers mean fewer nuts. When such a catastrophe occurs, squirrels must feed on less nutritious fare.

Gray squirrels of the forest are diurnal animals. This means they awaken at first light and spend these early hours feeding, grooming, foraging, and playing. When midday arrives, all activity ceases. Many squirrels go to their nests to sleep, but you might see some stretched out on tree branches or other perches. In late afternoon the pace picks up again. You can hear the chatter, buzz, and purrs of the gray squirrels as they tear along the forest floor. The playful squirrels must remain alert or they may become meals for predatory foxes, hawks, weasels, and tree-climbing snakes.

Life in the city is somewhat different. Squirrels have had to adjust their hours of activity and skip a midday siesta whenever they hear the rustle of a lunch bag. Just try to eat a solitary lunch in the park.

The gray squirrel has probably been around for about twenty-eight million years, yet we know very little about them. As the pace of mammal research picks up, we can hope to learn more about one of our favorite mammals.

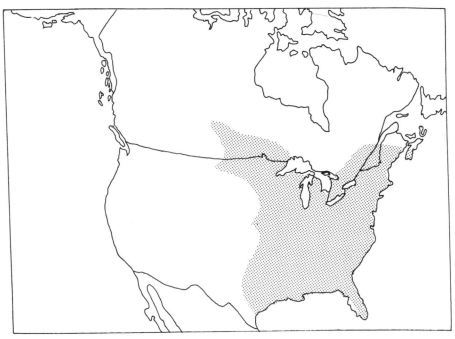

The range of the eastern gray squirrel (Sciurus carolinensis) *covers most of the eastern half of North America.*

THE CANOPY

THE WORLD OF GRAY SQUIRRELS

What to Bring	Science Skills
notebook	*observing*
pencil	*recording*
binoculars	*measuring*
watch with second hand	*comparing*
ruler	
crayons	
a sense of humor	

OBSERVATIONS

A Look at Squirrels. Observe a squirrel as it moves over the ground. Does it walk or hop? Does it move in a series of jerky starts and stops? An alert squirrel can remain motionless for long periods of time. What is the longest "pause" you have observed?

A Closer Look. How gray is the gray squirrel? A pair of binoculars will

A bushy tail helps the gray squirrel to keep its balance while moving through the forest canopy.

The gray squirrel grows tufts of white hair behind its ears in the winter. It has four sharp incisors—two above and two below—with a distinct gap between these teeth and the grinding teeth.

help you get a close look at the squirrel's fur. What colors do you see? Trace an outline of a squirrel and color it appropriately.

How does the color of the fur on the squirrel's back differ from the color of its belly? What is the advantage of this color pattern to the squirrel? (See Chapter Note 1, on color and countershading.)

Observe the gray squirrel throughout the year. What changes do you observe? During the winter look for the tufts of fur that grow behind the ears of the gray squirrel. For how many months can you see the tufts? (See Chapter Note 2, on fur.)

Markings and behaviors help you distinguish one squirrel from another. Learn to identify a particular squirrel. What characteristics do you use?

A Squirrel's Tail. A squirrel's tail serves as a blanket during the cold winter months and shades the squirrel from the summer sun. It is essential to the squirrel's acrobatic success.

How long is the squirrel's tail? Is it longer or shorter than the squirrel body, or the same length? (See Chapter Note 3, on squirrel size.)

How does a squirrel use its tail as it leaps from tree to tree? As the squirrel runs along a fence or stone wall, does it hold its tail up in the air or move it from side to side? Does the squirrel hold its tail directly behind its body during these maneuvers? Since squirrels can move quickly (up to fifteen miles per hour), you will want to check your observations by watching more than one squirrel.

Squirrel Grooming. Squirrels are not the fussy groomers cats are, but they do take special care of their tails. Watch the squirrel groom its tail. How long does it take? Does the squirrel follow any particular pattern, or is the cleaning a haphazard process?

Squirrel Talk. Squirrels are very vocal; they growl, gurgle, purr, buzz, and chatter. As you walk in the woods or in a wooded park, listen for squirrel noises. People often assume that many squirrel noises are made by birds.

Squirrel sounds are often accompanied by tail waving or tail flicking. Can you infer from these behaviors what the sounds mean? Consider danger, anger, and excitement.

Popsicles and Other Goodies. In March, when the sap in the trees begins to flow, look for squirrels chewing on sap icicles that formed during the night. They love the sweet taste of sap, especially from sugar maples.

Look for squirrels eating the tender young leaves of oaks and maples, and the blossoms of shagbark hickories and elms.

Squirrel Nests. A squirrel's winter home is usually the dry hollow of an abandoned woodpecker hole. Look for these nests especially in oak or beech trees. The nest is lined with grass, moss, and shredded leaves. Nests in tree hollows are used for breeding and raising the first litter of three or four young squirrels.

Do the squirrels make their nests in the same trees during successive winters?

Squirrels must leave the nest every two or three days during the cold months to forage for food. What time of the day do they leave the nest and look for food during the winter? Where do they go? (If you discover a place where squirrels have hidden their nuts, do not remove them.) Do the squirrels eat the nuts as they dig them up, or do they bring the nuts back to the nest?

Squirrels also build dreys, or leaf nests, firmly anchored in the crotch of a tree. People often assume they were built by large birds. Dreys serve as summer nests, and squirrels often raise a second litter in them.

To build a drey, the squirrel first weaves stout twigs and branches together to make a sturdy platform. Then it gathers leaves, grass, and moss to line the nest and build the sides. A roof of woven twigs and leaves protects the occupants from rain and sun. The completed ball is about two feet across. Seen from the ground, it looks like a haphazard mess of leaves. An industrious

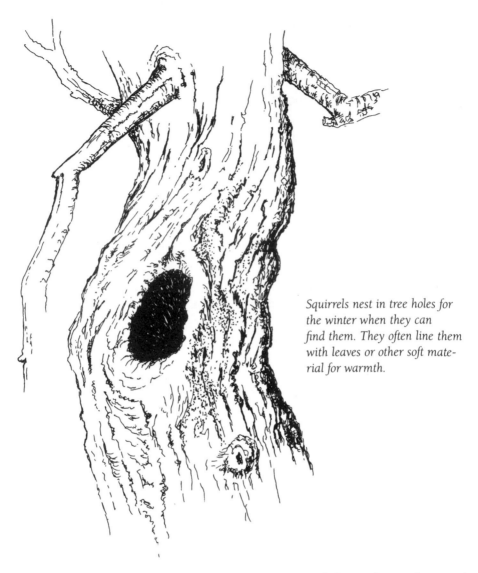

Squirrels nest in tree holes for the winter when they can find them. They often line them with leaves or other soft material for warmth.

squirrel can complete a drey in four or five days. Look for evidence of squirrel families in these dreys.

A third type of nest, built near the tips of the branches, is not as well constructed as the other kind of leaf nest. These summer dreys serve as bachelor pads, each occupied by a lone male squirrel. Males take no part in raising the young, nor do they do any household chores. Can you spot this squirrel as it enters and leaves the summer drey?

When taking a trip by car, count how many squirrel nests you see. How many nests can you find in three miles? In five miles?

The young are raised in summer dreys, or nests.

Squirrel Claws. Cats and squirrels can both climb trees. But have you ever seen a squirrel back down a tree trunk? Squirrels have a neat adaptation that makes coming down as easy as going up. Can you discover it? A squirrel sensing danger on its way down the tree trunk will freeze. This is a good time to look at its paws. (See Chapter Note 4, on claws.)

EXPLORATIONS

Legs for Jumping. Squirrels are well adapted for life in the trees. They have sharp claws for climbing and hanging, and sturdy, muscular hind legs for

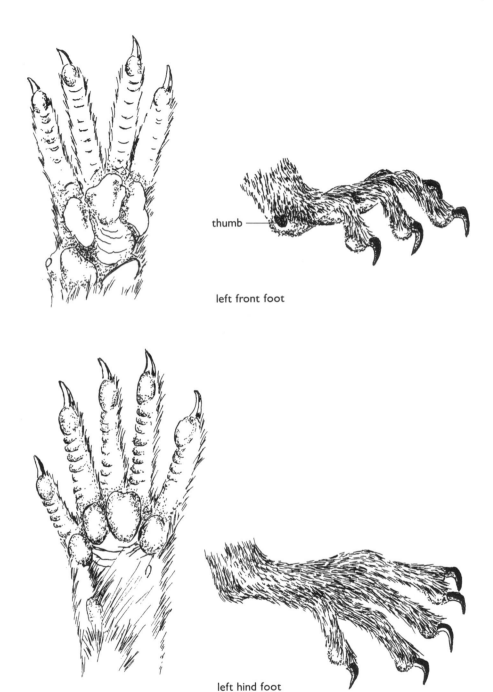

thumb

left front foot

left hind foot

The gray squirrel's feet are well adapted for climbing up and down trees. The soles of its hind feet are often furred in winter.

THE CANOPY

tree squirrel

flying squirrel

prairie dogs

ground squirrel

woodchuck or marmot

chipmunk

Squirrels (Sciuridae), of the order Rodentia, all have four toes on each front foot and five on each hind foot. The tail is always covered with hair.

jumping. One squirrel-leaping record is an amazing sixty feet. Watch several squirrels as they leap from place to place. Estimate the average distance your squirrels can jump.

Squirrel Pathways. Find a squirrel nest and watch it for some time. Do the squirrels leave and return to the nest by way of the same path?

Are the paths always along the ground, or are some in the treetops? Does more than one squirrel use a trail? Make a map showing the trails of the different squirrels that live in the nest.

How Close Is Too Close? How close can you get to a squirrel before it scampers away? Does it make a difference from which direction you approach the squirrel? Try approaching several squirrels from different directions. What did you find out? Do urban squirrels allow you to get closer to them than woodland squirrels?

How do squirrels react when approached by other squirrels? Do they fight or chase? Do they ignore each other? How close will one squirrel allow another to approach before reacting?

CHAPTER NOTES

1. **Squirrel Color and Countershading.** The gray squirrel appears gray, but one scientist has identified twenty-seven colors and shadings in the pelt of the gray squirrel. He failed to find a purely gray hair but instead found hairs with bands of black, white, and brown. These blend to give the appearance of gray. Look closely for the russet, cinnamon, and golden hues in the squirrel's pelt.

There is no gray at all on the squirrel's white underside. *Countershading* is the term given to their special kind of camouflage, which helps conceal squirrels when they are in trees. The light color on the underside makes it difficult for a predator, looking up, to see its prey. Looking down into the tree, it is equally difficult to see the darker gray of the squirrel back. Countershading protects the squirrels from flying predators, such as hawks, and from earthbound predators, like hunters.

2. **Squirrel Fur.** Squirrels molt twice each year. During the winter months, the outer layer of the squirrel's pelt consists of smooth, coarse hair. The inner layer of fine, downlike fur traps air, insulating the squirrel from the damp cold of winter. Beneath the fine fur, just below the skin, is a layer of fat that further protects the squirrel. Thus far, no one has determined the role of the ear tufts. The squirrel's sleek spring coat is a lighter shade of gray than the thick pelage of winter.

house cat

gray squirrel

red squirrel

domestic dog

Learning to distinguish common animal tracks is relatively easy. The tracks of all common squirrels show four toes on the front track and five toes on the hind track. When squirrels move, their hind feet land in front of their forefeet—a type of movement called galloping.

3. Squirrel Size. The total length of the gray squirrel ranges from fourteen inches to about twenty inches. Of that length, the tail measures seven to ten inches. A gray squirrel weighs anywhere from three-quarters of a pound to one and a half pounds.

4. Squirrel Claws. Cat claws are arranged for going up tree trunks. To get down a cat must either jump or creep backward down the trunk. Squirrels' paws have an adaptation that solves this problem. Squirrels can turn their paws 180 degrees, so their claws are always in the ideal grasping position, even on the way down.

CHAPTER 5

Starlings

HOW TO BEAT THE ODDS

About one hundred years ago a New Yorker, Eugene Schiefelin, decided to bring a little of the Old World to America. He thought it would be a good idea to import from England all the birds mentioned in the plays of Shakespeare. The European starling (*Sturnus vulgaris*) was one of those birds.

In each of two successive years, Schiefelin released about eighty European starlings in New York City. From that modest beginning the birds have spread across North America. You can find them from northern Mexico to James Bay, Canada, from New York to Alaska, and every place in between. Of the estimated six hundred million starlings worldwide, one third of them live in North America. The European starling has conquered its new land.

The key to the starling's success is that it can take over niches previously filled by other birds. Starlings have many behavioral and structural advantages that make these takeovers possible.

Starlings are strong, aggressive birds. In the many reports of fights between them and other birds, starlings seldom lose. Their sharp beaks often leave telltale marks on the victims. If a starling needs a place to live, it simply appropriates a nest occupied by another bird. Starlings are not intimidated even by large birds. Using their strength and cunning, starlings are usually able to evict the owner. They have been known to push flickers, considerably larger birds, out of their nests. If there are eggs in the coveted nest, the new tenants throw them out, too.

Although starlings prefer natural cavities, they will take shelter in your mailbox, in the vents of your attic, or even in a convenient drainpipe. This willingness to nest almost anywhere under all kinds of conditions contributes to their success.

Though most cavity nesters are satisfied with a thin bed of feathers, starlings make their nests of grasses. Most of the grasses are dry, but some are young green shoots containing antiparasitic chemicals. The nest remains hygienic even after the hatchlings arrive. The fastidious parents remove fecal sacs from the nests as soon as the young deposit them. Yet as soon as the young develop their feathers, housekeeping ends; parasites move in and claim the nest. The number of parasites that starlings can tolerate without an increase in their mortality is amazing.

Starlings breed in large groups. Within these colonies the males seek out females that have successfully raised large numbers of fledglings. Males often mate more than once during the breeding season. This further guarantees a large crop of starlings. Sometimes this second or even third mating is with a different female. Each clutch generally has four to six eggs.

Other adaptations have helped the starlings do well in their new land. A glance at their slender, tapered bill suggests that starlings probe for their food. But the special design of the muscles that control the bill allow starlings to forage differently from other kinds of birds. Most birds have strong muscles designed for snapping the lower bill shut, but the muscles that control the beaks of starlings work in a slightly different way. The primary strength of their muscles is used to open the bill with force. With this "spring action" the bird can move objects such as small rocks and can make sizable holes in compacted soil.

Open-bill probing, or gaping, is the name given to this technique. Because of it, starlings can hunt for spiders, grubs, and other delicacies that live beneath the surface of the ground. If you look carefully at a foraging starling, you can see the rhythmic stab and open, stab and open of the working bill. The yellow-headed blackbird and the brown-headed cowbird also use the open-bill probing technique.

Starling vision also contributes to their survival. Starlings can move each eye independently of the other, forward, backward, up, and down. This helps the bird look out for predators. These visual adaptations are also useful when the birds probe for food. The bird can move its eyes forward and peer into the hole to see what's available. This binocular vision eliminates the need for the starling to cock its head from side to side as other birds must do.

People in some communities are not impressed with the success of the European starling. The citizens of one town used everything they could think of to rid themselves of 150,000 starlings. They tried bombarding the roost site with loud noises from shotgun blasts, firecrackers, and loudspeakers. The birds didn't budge. Other communities have thought of using chemicals for starling birth control. The problem with that idea was that there was no way to keep other bird species from being treated. *Sturnus vulgaris* does not discourage easily.

THE WORLD OF STARLINGS

What to Bring	Science Skills
binoculars	observing
notebook	recording
pen or pencil	

OBSERVATIONS

A Look at Starlings. During the fall and winter look for the starling's speckled plumage. The buff-white dots you see at this time are the tips of

The European starling (Sturnus vulgaris) *exhibits this striking plumage only in winter.*

the bird's feathers. Do you think these dots look like stars? Could that be the reason for the bird's common name?

In the spring the white stars give way to the iridescent sheen of the breeding plumage. The feathers have not changed color; through exposure to sunlight and physical wear and tear, the white tips have worn away. The male house sparrow *(Passer domesticus)* develops its nuptial black bib through the same process. The black color is a result of the wearing away of the buff-colored tips on those feathers.

Starlings have a complete molt once each year. The process begins late in July, after the mating season, and continues into the fall. Look for these birds in their starry winter garb as the trees begin to change color.

The starling's bill also changes color. During the fall the bill fades from the bright yellow of the breeding season to a dull brown. It remains this color throughout the winter.

Watch an individual bird as it forages. You will see the rhythmic action of the bill as it stabs and opens the ground to expose the insects below. You may want to use binoculars to get a better look.

Watch a starling move from one place to another. How would you describe its gait? Does it hop or does it walk or strut?

Sometimes the angle of the light prevents you from seeing the color of a bird's feathers or other details you rely on for identification. Learning to recognize a bird's shape against a gray sky or other drab background can be very helpful. Starlings differ from other birds of their size in that they have a very short tail. Drawing birds in silhouette illustrates this characteristic and lets you compare starlings with other birds of various sizes.

A Feeding Flock. Starlings forage in flocks. The number of birds in any one of these flocks can vary from ten to several hundred. Find some of these feeding flocks. How many birds were there in each flock? What is the average number of birds in the flocks you found?

What is the advantage of foraging in flocks as compared with solitary feeding? (See Chapter Note 1, on flock feeding.) Make your own observations of the behavior of starlings feeding alone and those found in flocks of various sizes. Compare your findings with those of the field investigators.

Organization Within the Flock. If you observe a flock of starlings as they forage, you will see that they are not scattered haphazardly over the field. There is an order to their activity. Can you discover the pattern of organization? (See Chapter Note 2, on organization.)

People have described a flock of foraging starlings as "rolling" across the field. When the birds foraging at the back of the flock are finished, they fly low over the flock to the front. This leapfrog pattern is repeated throughout the feeding.

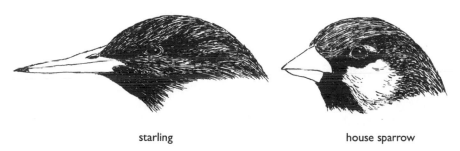

starling   house sparrow

Male starlings and house sparrows both display special spring, or nuptial, plumage.

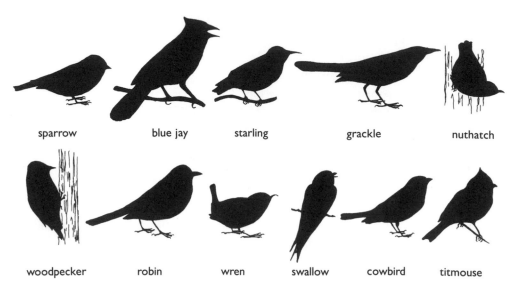

sparrow	blue jay	starling	grackle	nuthatch

woodpecker	robin	wren	swallow	cowbird	titmouse

An observer often has only a bird's silhouette by which to identify it. Use this table to help identify these common birds.

A flock of birds flying in tight formation is less likely to be attacked by predators. Look for a group of birds flying in loose formation. How long does it take for the flock to tighten its ranks if a hawk is in the area? Describe the behavior of the flock. How does the hawk respond?

Pre-roosting Behavior. Late in the afternoon, while some of the pale light of the winter day remains, starlings leave their feeding grounds and congregate in larger groups. The places where these groups meet are called staging areas. Look for staging areas in your neighborhood. How many can you find? Sometimes these staging groups pick up additional birds as they fly to the roost. Have you seen any of these airborne hitchhikers join the flock?

If you would like to learn some methods for estimating the number of birds in a flying flock, *The Audubon Society Handbook for Birders* by Stephen W. Kress (see the bibliography) gives some excellent suggestions.

Roosting Behavior. Starlings form large groups that spend the night together. What is the advantage of this? (See Chapter Note 3, on roosting.)

Many roosts are enormous and may contain starlings and other blackbirds. Can you identify some of the other birds in the roost? (See Chapter Note 4 for some staggering statistics.) How many birds are there in some of the roosts in your neighborhood?

Try to be near a roost on several different days when the birds arrive. Is there a pattern to the way the birds approach the roost? Do all the birds fly in from the same direction each day? Do all the birds enter the roost at the same time?

Starling Hygiene. Starlings don't limit themselves to bathing in water. They also engage in a process called anting. In this activity the bird captures an ant of a species that secrets formic acid and strokes the ant along its feathers, paying special attention to its wings, rump, and tail. Often the birds twist and turn as they do this, and it is not unusual for a bird to tumble over itself while cleaning.

Look for starlings anting. Is there a sequence to the process? How long does it take for a bird to complete the job?

No one knows exactly why birds do this, but several explanations have been given. One suggestion is that the formic acid secreted by ants kills bird parasites.

CHAPTER NOTES

1. **Flock Feeding.** Birds that feed in groups can spend more time feeding and less time looking for predators. One researcher discovered that a bird feeding alone spent fifty percent of the time looking up for predators and fifty percent of the time feeding. When five birds were in the feeding group, individuals could spend seventy percent of the time feeding. Ten birds in the flock increased feeding time to ninety percent for each bird.

The scientists who collected this information did exactly what you are doing. They sat, watched, and recorded what they saw in their field notebooks.

2. **Flock Organization.** Scientists have discovered that in the spring, starlings forage in male-female pairs. Look closely and you'll probably see this behavior. Although it's impossible for an observer to distinguish the sexes of the birds, you can infer that the pairs you see are composed of a male and a female starling. The two birds don't feed side by side. Instead the female feeds in front of the male. The birds in the pair are generally not more than a foot apart. If the birds get too far apart, another male may try to capture the female for himself. When this happens, a scuffle usually occurs.

3. **Roosting.** Roosting is another strategy that protects the birds from predators. Because they don't see well in the dark, starlings are especially at risk at night. The collective eye of the flock serves all the members better than any one pair.

Cramming together in trees, under highway bridges, or in deserted buildings has additional benefits. The surface area of individual birds exposed to the freezing rain and killing winds of winter is reduced. Thus the energy stores of each bird are conserved.

4. Roosting Statistics. One roost in Texas was reported to contain fifty million birds. Another discovered in Virginia had twenty-five million birds, and a Louisiana roost held twenty-one million birds.

Starlings were not the only birds in these roosts. Other birds included red-winged blackbirds, grackles, brown-headed cowbirds, rusty blackbirds, boat-tailed grackles, yellow-headed blackbirds, and red-eyed cowbirds. Look for some of these birds in the roosts near your home.

PART II

THE FIELD

M OST OF THE LARGE FIELDS and meadows we see today were once prosperous farmlands. Some field areas were never cultivated. For various reasons, trees in these areas have been eliminated or have not survived or have been very slow to take over. Sometimes a field exists because the soil is sandy or because it has large, underlying areas of rock. It may lack adequate amounts of life-sustaining nutrients for trees. Such open places are home to a special group of plants and animals.

The reason fields are special habitats is the lack of shade. Fields receive direct sunlight at ground level. This makes them hot. Sunlight also causes rapid evaporation of moisture. The acid and mineral content of the soil may vary from place to place. These conditions all have an effect on plant and animal life. In the following chapters, you will meet some of the various life forms typical of this habitat.

CHAPTER 6

Wildflowers

BEAUTIFUL WEEDS

For thousands of years farmers have been sowing the seeds of edible plants. For just as long they have been bothered by plants they did not want sprouting in their fields. But what the farmer considers weeds, a homeowner may cultivate as wildflowers.

Not all wildflowers grow everywhere. Habitat conditions and hereditary traits team up to determine where particular kinds of wildflowers will flourish. The physical characteristics of a habitat—variables as temperature, moisture, light, wind, soil type, and the topography of the land—influence its suitability for a wildflower species. Even within a habitat some wildflowers tolerate wildly fluctuating physical conditions, while others are sensitive to the slightest variations. Many wildflowers have adapted to some of the earth's most extreme environmental conditions.

The inhospitable desert of the American southwest is one of those habitats. During the day, desert plants suffer relentless heat; at night they're in the grip of sudden cold. Other wildflowers make their homes in more moderate habitats—shaded woodlands cooled by meandering steams or sunny fields and pastures.

Each habitat presents a unique set of problems for the plants that live there. Let's take a look at some of the problems for plants living in fields and meadows and see how they've adapted.

The leaves and stems of many plants living in open fields are covered with tiny hairs. These hairs effectively reduce air flow over the surface of the plant, which minimizes water loss through evaporation. Plants growing in this dry environment also have smaller and thicker leaves than wildflowers in moister environments.

Meadow-dwelling plants have root systems designed for areas with limited water. The shallow, spreading root of chickweeds can absorb surface water quickly. Many wildflowers that grow in poor, sandy soils have long taproots that reach deep into the earth in search of water.

Grazing animals present another problem, especially for plants that grow in pastures. Many of these wildflowers are protected from grazing animals by a coat of unpleasant-tasting fuzz. Still other plants of pastureland sport stout thorns on their stems and sharp spines on their leaves. Thistles (*Cirsium* sp.) have adopted this strategy.

The familiar dandelion produces a flat circle of leaves that hugs the ground. This structure, called a basal rosette, maximizes the use of available sunlight and offers protection from the cold of winter. In their flattened position on the ground, the leaves not only find shelter in the "dead" air space but also utilize

Common knotweed forms a circular mat with shallow, spreading roots.

the heat that was stored in the ground during the summer. Furthermore, with the basal rosette only the upper surface of the leaf is exposed to the weather. The leaves of many basal rosettes are hairy. Common mullein and teasel, two very common plants of field and roadside, have basal rosettes.

Botanists often group wildflowers into three major categories based on their life cycles: annuals, biennials, and perennials. In any recently disturbed field the first wildflowers to appear are annuals. The following year the biennials arrive and the year after that, the perennials.

Annuals are those plants that grow, produce and disperse seeds, and die in one season. The next generation survives the winter as dormant seeds, which will germinate in the spring if conditions are right. You can expect to find annuals in freshly cleared areas. Daisy fleabane (*Erigeron annuus*), common sow thistle (*Sonchus oleraceus*), and fringed gentian (*Gentiana crinita*) are typical. The annual cocklebur (*Xanthium* sp.) has developed an ingenious reproductive strategy. The plant produces burs that contain two seeds. One of the seeds in each bur germinates the first year. The other requires more oxygen to germinate and remains dormant until the second year. Thus, one plant can produce two generations of cocklebur.

You can expect to find many biennials growing in young fields as well.

Biennials live for two years. In the first year they develop leaves, stems, and root systems, which are sustained throughout the winter. A few biennials, such as common mullein, teasel, and common burdock, spend the winter as a basal rosette.

In the second year the biennial puts its energy into flower production and seed manufacture. Queen Anne's Lace (*Daucus carota*), common burdock (*Arctium minus*), bull thistle (*Cirsium vulgare*), and wild lettuce (*Lactuca canadensis*), are among the biennials you can expect to find in older fields.

Most wildflowers are perennials. A perennial spends a great deal of its first-year energy budget producing a tough, rugged plant that can withstand harsh winter winds, freezing temperatures, long periods of darkness, and extended drought.

Protected by the warmth held within the soil, the roots of established perennials wait for spring. Many of the roots will produce flower-bearing shoots. At the end of the growing season, the flowers will yield a crop of seeds dispersed by a variety of methods.

When you see a field filled with perennials such as goldenrod, white field asters, and tansy (*Tanacetum vulgare*), you are looking at a maturing field. Bouncing bet (*Saponaria officinalis*), and common St. Johnswort (*Hypericum perforatum*) are also found in older fields. This sequence of annual to biennial to perennial, however, is only a general outline of the development of wildflowers in an abandoned field. Nature is seldom this tidy.

Wildflowers illustrate very well that the study of nature is the study of survival techniques. Strategies that work in one place don't work in another. What works one year may not be suitable the next. Nature responds to the most subtle of changes, so we need to be aware that our modifications of the habitats around us can have a profound effect on the things living there.

THE WORLD OF WILDFLOWERS

What to Bring	Science Skills
basic kit	*comparing*
camera	*measuring*
string	*predicting*
graph paper	

OBSERVATIONS

Great satisfactions come when you discover the variety of adaptations plants have evolved to permit them to thrive in different habitats. In the following activities you will get to see some of these clever survival tricks.

Some Adaptations of Common Wild Plants. The wildflowers discussed below are easily found along roadsides, in vacant lots, and in abandoned construction sites, as well as in fields.

Common Burdock (*Arctium minus*). This biennial is identified by its seed-filled burs, which remain on the plant throughout the winter. Look for burdock in rich soils along roadsides and in fallow farmlands.

Are there any plants growing beneath the burdock? How large an area is shaded by its leaves? How does the plant avoid shading its own leaves?

Do all the leaves grow from the stem at the same angle? Are the little stems (petioles) that attach the leaves to the main stem the same length? Are all the leaves on the plant the same size?

Canada Thistle (*Cirsium arvense*). Thistle is an aggressive plant. Its

Common burdock (Arctium minus) *is a biennial commonly found in older, more mature fields.*

The spines of Canada thistle (Cirsium arvense) *constitute an effective defense strategy.*

rapidly-creeping, underground stems (rhizomes) can produce new shoots. Be careful not to discard carelessly pieces of rhizomes; each piece can produce a new plant. Thistle is a serious nuisance in cultivated fields and pastures.

Its armor of sharp protective spines discourages grazing animals. In this way thistle lives long enough to produce and disperse seeds. The wind catches the floss attached to the seeds and carries them to new ground. You can find various species of thistle growing from June through October.

Dandelion *(Taraxacum officinale)*. This low-growing wildflower is common to fields and lawns. How are the leaves arranged? What is their shape? Look at its stalk. Do all dandelions have stalks the same length? Is the stalk solid? Does the length of the stalk depend on where it grows? Compare the stalks of field dandelions with those growing in lawns. How do you explain the difference?

Observe several dandelions at regular intervals during a day. What happens to them? When do the blossoms open and when do they close? Is there a difference between sunny days and cloudy days? How long do they stay open?

Watch several flower heads until the seeds are formed. How long does it take for this to happen? Remove some seeds and their silken parachutes. With a magnifier, take a close look at them. How many seeds are there in a flower head? Compare the dispersal strategy of these seeds with the seeds of other wildflowers.

The dandelion root is another key to its success. Dig up a dandelion and discover for yourself the secrets that dandelions hide beneath the soil.

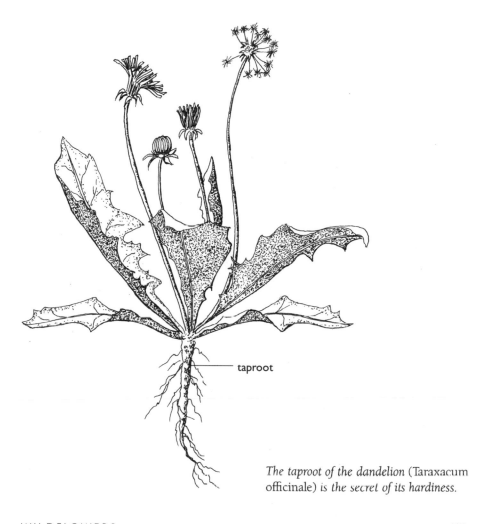

The taproot of the dandelion (Taraxacum officinale) *is the secret of its hardiness.*

Yarrow (*Achillea millefolium*). This is a pretty perennial that graces road-sides and fields. Dig up a yarrow plant to see its substantial system of underground stems. Yarrow reproduces asexually by producing new shoots along these underground stems.

Its stiff stems are hairy. This fuzz and the fernlike leaves with their smaller surface area help reduce water loss through evaporation.

Crush some of its leaves and smell the fragrance. When cows graze on yarrow, their milk tastes bitter.

Queen Anne's Lace (*Daucus carota*). This biennial is equipped with a thick taproot. The root has a dual purpose: It finds water below the soil surface and at the end of its first growing season, it stores nutrients for use during the

Yarrow (Achillea millefolium) *is an attractive perennial.*

Queen Anne's lace (Daucus carota) *has a substantial root system.*

winter. Carefully dig up the plant and examine the taproot. How long is it? Are there smaller roots growing from the taproot? Smell the taproot. The odor will give you a clue to the plant's informal name—wild carrot. When you are finished, replant your specimen.

Are the stems smooth or bristly? Describe the leaves. How are they de-signed to conserve water?

Now that you have had a little practice, look at some other wildflowers to discover their secrets for success.

Patterns in Flower Clusters. Botanists use a variety of clues to determine the identity of an unknown wildflower. One clue is the arrangement of the florets—tiny flowers that make up the cluster—or inflorescence.

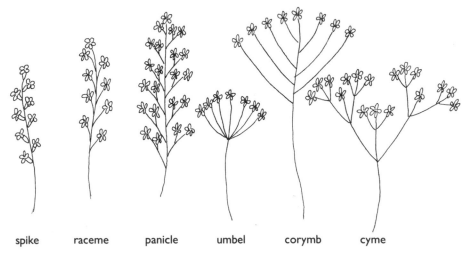

spike raceme panicle umbel corymb cyme

The arrangement of florets on a wildflower is a useful clue to its identity.

Spike. Florets grow singly on a tiny stem and appear like steps along the spike. Example: blue vervain *(Verbena hastata)*.

Raceme. Florets grow in steps along the stem but are attached to the stem by a tiny stalk. Example: wild lupine *(Lupinus perennis)*.

Panicle. The central stem of the cluster has alternate branches, each of which has smaller alternate branches. The florets grow at the ends of the branches. If you look carefully, you'll see that a panicle is a raceme whose branches have little branches. Example: Canada goldenrod *(Solidago canadensis)*.

Corymb. Each floret-bearing branch off the main stem is longer than the one above it. This produces a flat-topped flower cluster. Example: yarrow *(Achillea millefolium)*.

Umbel. A flat-topped pattern in which the flower stalks all grow from the same point on the stem. In a compound umbel several small flower stalks grow from the tips of the main stalks. Example: Queen Anne's lace *(Daucus carota)*.

Cyme. A flat-topped pattern in which branches off the main stem are opposite each other with a flower at each tip. Between the two branches is another flower, generally older than those on the branches. Example: campion.

EXPLORATIONS

From Flower to Seed. Wildflowers don't all bloom during the same time. Record blooming times for some common wildflowers in your neighborhood.

Which wildflowers bloom over the longest period of time? Which bloom for the shortest?

BLOOMING TIMES

Wildflower	Months							
	M	A	M	J	J	A	S	O
Black-eyed Susan (*Rudbeckia hirta*)				●━━━━━━━━━━●				
Rabbits-foot clover (*Trifolium arvense*)			●━━━━━━━━━━━━━●					
Canada thistle (*Cirsium arvense*)					●━━━━●			
Chicory (*Cichorium intybus*)				●━━━━━━━━━●				
Butterfly weed (*Asclepias tuberosa*)				●━━━━●				
Common St. Johnswort (*Hypericum perforatum*)				●━━●				

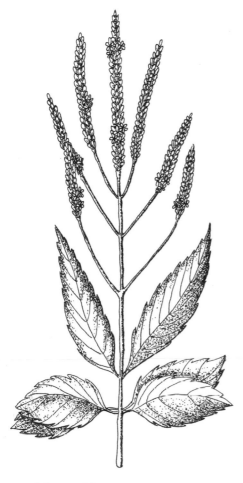

The florets of blue vervain (Verbena hastata) *open in staggered fashion.*

Do All the Florets in a Cluster Open at Once? An umbel of Queen Anne's lace is a cluster of tiny florets. Do all the florets in an umbel open at the same time or is the opening of the florets staggered? Do all the florets in the cluster wither at the same time?

Now look at some spike flowers, such as blue bervane and speedwell. The florets on these flower spikes do not open at the same time. Do those at the tip or the base of the spike open first? How long does it take for all the florets on the spike to open? (See Chapter Note 2, on patterns.)

The Effects of Daylight. The blossoms of some wildflowers, such as bindweed and dandelion, do not always remain open. These flowers open and close in a pattern dictated by the hours of daylight. Find some of these very common wildflowers and observe them for several days. What time do they open? What time do they close? How do they respond on a cloudy day?

Can you fool these plants into thinking their day is over sooner than it really is? A few hours after they have opened in the morning, cover the blooms of several dandelions with old coffee cans. How long does it take for the flower to close?

Try a similar investigation on bindweed. What did you find out?

Organizations for Wildflower Lovers. Wildflowers are among our most beloved botanical treasures. Associations committed to education about wildflowers and their preservation exist in almost every state. Call the extension service of your state university for help locating the groups in your area.

CHAPTER NOTES

1. Types of Reproduction in Flowering Plants. Plants can reproduce sexually or nonsexually (asexually). In the process of sexual reproduction, each of two "parent" plants contributes genetic material to the offspring. The pollen, or male reproductive cells, develop in the anthers of the stamen (the male portion of the flower); the female reproductive cells are produced in the ovary of the pistil (the female portion of the flower). When pollen fertilizes an egg, the resulting cell becomes a seed. The developing seed produces a new plant that is genetically different from either of the parents.

In nonsexual reproduction only one parent contributes all of the genetic material to the offspring. Plants can reproduce in this way by sending out underground shoots, which we call rhizomes. The shoots develop into new individuals exactly like the parent. Offspring produced in this way are called clones.

2. Blooming Patterns. The florets on the spike of blue vervain and some other wildflowers open first at the base of the spike and continue opening toward the tip until all have opened. All florets on the spike are not in bloom at the same time.

Other flowers begin to bloom at the middle of the spike. The florets then open toward the tip and toward the base of the spike simultaneously. See if you can find wildflowers that illustrate some of these interesting patterns.

CHAPTER 7

Goldenrod

THERE'S GOLD IN THOSE MEADOWS

Goldenrod is one of the most beautiful flowers of late summer. Clusters of these sweet-smelling wildflowers stand tall above the fading green meadows. Their yellow hue alerts insects to vast stores of pollen and nectar. Nectar is the sweet liquid produced by flowers and stored in nectaries at their bases.

Goldenrod belongs to the daisy or composite (Compositae) family. This is the largest and perhaps most recently evolved group of flowering plants. Other members of this huge botanical clan include asters, yarrow, and chicory. Composites such as the oxeye daisy have one large, showy flower head, which encourages visits from syrphid flies, honeybees, and other pollinators. Goldenrod has a different strategy for ensuring pollination. Instead of one large flower, goldenrod has a flower head made up of many tiny yellow tufts. The tufts are set close together, producing a mass of alluring gold, which beckons insect pollinators.

Each tuft is made up of two different kinds of flowers. In the center of the tuft are the disk flowers, which have both male and female parts. Around the tuft lies a circle of flat "petals." These are ray flowers, each with only female parts. Both ray and disk flowers can produce seeds when pollinated. There can be from three to fifteen ray flowers in a single yellow tuft, depending on the species of goldenrod.

Botanists have assigned goldenrod to the genus *Solidago*, from the Latin meaning "to make whole or healthy." Goldenrod was once used as a medicine, but today many people mistakenly blame goldenrod for their hay fever. Goldenrod's bright, showy flowers produce heavy pollen, which sticks to the fuzzy bodies of bees, flies, and other feeding insects. Ragweed, grasses, and other plants with inconspicuous flowers produce light, dry pollen, which is dispersed by the wind. The pollen from these plants causes the allergic reaction we know as hay fever. Goldenrod is blamed because its flowers bloom at the same time and are so conspicuous.

It has been said that no other flower attracts as many kinds of insects as goldenrod. Longhorn and soldier beetles come to feed on the pollen. These beetles can be identified by their long thick antennae, which measure at least one half the length of the beetle's bodies. Their bright yellow, orange, and red markings contrast beautifully with the goldenrod flowers.

You'll find the goldenrod bouquet frequented by many tiny black or brown blister beetles. When disturbed, they secrete a foul-smelling, oily, toxic substance from their leg joints. This toxin can raise a nasty blister on the unwary naturalist, thus its name.

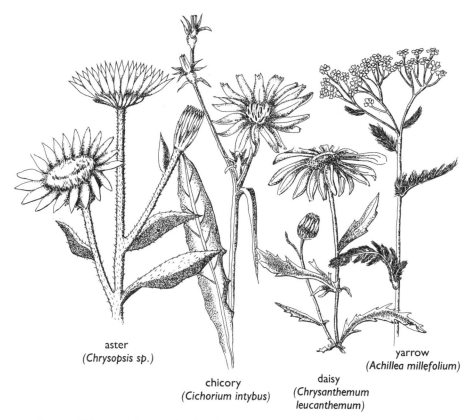

aster
(*Chrysopsis sp.*)

chicory
(*Cichorium intybus*)

daisy
(*Chrysanthemum
leucanthemum*)

yarrow
(*Achillea millefolium*)

These wildflowers belong to the family Compositae, which evolved fairly recently.

Other visitors include honeybees, butterflies, bumblebees, and syrphid flies. Next to bees, the less-well-known syrphid flies are the most important pollinators of goldenrod. Though they resemble wasps or bees, syrphid flies neither sting nor bite. They come for a sip of nectar and in turn pollinate the receptive ray and disk flowers.

The ambush bug, a predatory insect, is a frequent associate of goldenrod. Exquisitely camouflaged in yellow, with black or brown markings, this hunter lurks among the golden tufts waiting for unsuspecting bees, butterflies, or other pollinators. This usually sluggish bug has specially adapted legs, which move with lightening speed to snatch the prey. Its clawlike pincers deliver the death blow.

The ambush bug injects an enzyme into the body of the prey that causes the prey's internal organs to liquidize. The ambush bug sucks this "soup" up the way we drink soda through a straw. Only the rigid exoskeleton of the prey

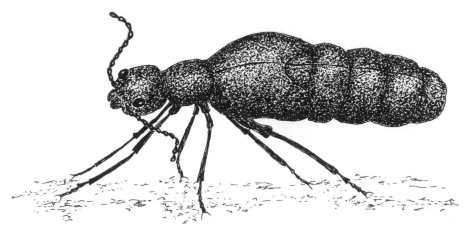

Blister beetles (family Meloidae) *are attracted to goldenrod.*

remains. Look carefully and you may see the vestiges of an ambush bug's victim on a goldenrod flower.

Another group of predatory arthropods that live among the goldenrod are crab spiders. This spider scuttles along sideways through the tufts of goldenrod and its two front claws are held in front of its body. These behaviors give it a crablike appearance.

The well-camouflaged crab spider has predatory habits and culinary tastes similar to those of ambush bugs, although its method of attack is quite different. Some of its fascinating characteristics are discussed in the next section of this book.

Walking in a field of goldenrod is one of late summer's pleasures. Enjoy the pungent, herbal smells of the meadow, but don't forget to take your hand lens, bug box, and notebook.

THE WORLD OF GOLDENROD

What to Bring	Science Skills
basic kit	*observing*
baby food jars with lids	*measuring*
string (100 feet)	*graphing*
rubbing alcohol	*recording*
small aquarium net	*comparing*
yellow paper	*inferring*
white paper	

OBSERVATIONS

Goldenrod can be found in a variety of sunny habitats. Look for it in fields and meadows, along railroad beds, and in vacant lots and roadside ditches.

The Goldenrod Clan. There are many different kinds of goldenrod and they interbreed. This causes confusion for the beginning naturalist as well as the expert.

Instead of trying to identify each kind of goldenrod you find, look for some general characteristics displayed by all the plants. The questions below will help you focus.

How are the flower clusters arranged? Are they flat-topped? Is the cluster long and narrow like a wand? Are they on one side of down-curved branchlets? Are the clusters thick and clublike toward the top or are they like plumes?

What is the shape of the leaves? Are they lancelike, or elliptical like a football? Are the leaf veins parallel to each other or are they branching? Are the leaves hairy? Are the leaf edges jagged or smooth?

Early goldenrod (*Solidago juncea*), rough-stemmed goldenrod (*S. rugosa*), gray goldenrod (*S. nemoralis*), and showy goldenrod (*S. speciosa*) are some of the types of goldenrod you can expect to find. Check your field guide to find out which goldenrods grow in your area.

Asexual Reproduction. Find a place where goldenrod is growing. Do you see a distribution pattern? Are the plants scattered randomly across the field or are they grouped together in clumps?

Is all the goldenrod in a clump the same kind? How do you know? What are the characteristics of the plants in the clump? Are the flower heads of each plant arranged in the same way on the stem? Do the leaves on different plants in the group have similar traits? Are the plants the same height?

Goldenrods have developed two reproductive strategies. One strategy involves a system of underground stems called rhizomes. In the fall each plant sends out rhizomes in a wagon-wheel pattern. New plants sprout from the tips of the rhizomes, forming a circular cluster of goldenrod plants.

Because this strategy does not involve the union of sex cells from two different parents, it is called asexual reproduction, and the offspring are called clones. Genetically speaking, the whole clump of clones is identical and can be considered one "plant." The advantage of this arrangement is that the plant can survive much longer than any of the individual stems in the cluster.

A Closer Look at Clones. Look between the stems of the individual clones. How much space is there between them? Do you find other kinds of plants growing among the clones? What advantage is this for the goldenrod? Do you find any groups of clones where the center plants are missing and

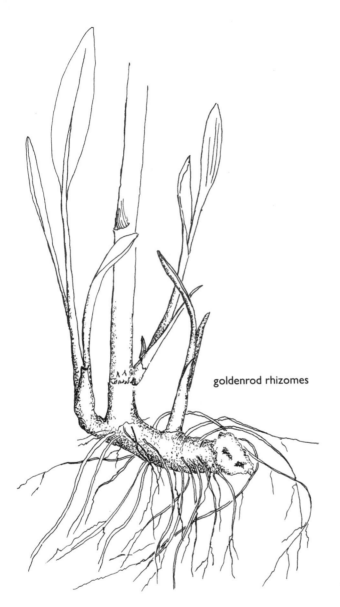

goldenrod rhizomes

Goldenrod reproduces by cloning itself.

the remaining plants form a circle around an empty space? How would you explain this?

Sexual Reproduction. Goldenrod's other method of reproduction yields seeds, which are the result of the union of gametes (male and female sex cells). In the fall a profusion of fuzzy seeds drop from the aging flowers. Because the seeds are very light, they are dispersed by the wind to places where they can begin new colonies.

The seeds germinate and produce only a leafy stem during their first year

THE FIELD

of growth. Flowers don't appear until the second year. Look for these leafy stems. Try to find one of these young plants and follow the sequence of development.

Goldenrod Visitors. Goldenrod is a rich source of energy for many insects and spiders. As you explore the stems, leaves, roots, and flowers of goldenrod, you will find creatures with special adaptations for sipping sap – the liquid that flows through a plant's vascular system – or for chewing leaves and stems. Some insects are specially colored to hide among the yellow flowers; these will require a more deliberate search.

Look for the special physical and behavioral adaptations of the insects and spiders that live in this fascinating community. The outline on the following page organizes the goldenrod menagerie according to their life-styles and indicates the part of the plant where you can expect to find them. This list is not a complete roll call of the insects and spiders that flock to goldenrod for nourishment and shelter. It is probably enough to get you started as you dive into the world of insects.

Camouflage and Crab Spiders. Crab spiders are particularly fascinating goldenrod associates because of their special adaptation for feeding on goldenrod. They've adopted the goldenrod's yellow color, so you may have to spend some time looking for one.

When you discover a crab spider, put it in a baby food jar or similar container lined with plain white paper. Poke some holes in the lid and secure it. You will be keeping your spider in the jar for a couple of days, so you'll have to feed it. Serve small flies or other tiny insects with a pair of tweezers. What color was the crab spider when you first put it into the jar? What happened to its color after a few days?

Put the same crab spider into another baby food jar, this one lined with yellow paper. Secure the lid. Wait another few days and feed as necessary. What happened to the color of the crab spider this time? How is this adaptation helpful to the crab spider?

Succession in a Field. Under ordinary conditions, neglected fields and meadows will pass through predictable stages called succession. Fields of grasses and wildflowers will yield to larger plants, such as vines and shrubs, and ultimately will give way to trees. The woodland is a relatively stable state called a climax; only certain plant diseases, insect invasions, fires, or human interference will alter the woodland system. The number of years it takes to reach this climax can usually be estimated with considerable accuracy.

Fields with goldenrod, however, do not proceed along this path according to a predictable timetable. Instead, goldenrod meadows remain in the field condition for a very long time, perhaps fifty years or so. This happens because

THE GOLDENROD MENAGERIE

HERBIVORES	**PREDATORS**
LEAF EATERS	SPIDERS
tree-hoppers (*Homoptera*)	harvestmen (daddy longlegs) (*Phalangium*)
goldenrod beetles (*Coleoptera*)	garden spiders (*Argiopidae*)
NECTAR DRINKERS	banded Argiope
honeybees (*Hymenoptera*)	black-and-yellow Argiope
carpenter bees (*Hymenoptera*)	crab spiders (*Thomisidae*)
bumblebees (*Hymenoptera*)	INSECT PREDATORS
wasps (*Hymenoptera*)	assassin bug (*Reduviidae*)
hover flies (*Diptera*)	ambush bug (*Phymatidae*)
moths (*Lepidoptera*)	
butterflies (*Lepidoptera*)	
FLOWER EATERS Japanese beetle (*Popillia japonica*)	
SAP SIPPERS	
bugs (*Hemiptera*)	
aphids, hoppers, and lacewings (*Homoptera*)	
POLLEN EATERS	
adult locust borer (*Coleoptera*)	
adult black blister beetle (*Coleoptera*)	
paper wasp (*Hymenoptera*)	

goldenrods produce chemicals that repress the growth of larger plants that would ordinarily move into a field quite easily.

Monitor a field with goldenrod and one without it. Record your observations for each field and see what happens. This is a very long range project, but it only requires one or two observations during each growing season. Who knows what else you might discover?

The chart on the next three pages will help you identify some frequent goldenrod visitors.

Order	Some representatives	Traits	Eating style
Hemiptera	Ambush bugs, assassin bugs	All adults have wings. A large triangle is usually visible between the base of the forward wings.	Piercing, sucking
Homoptera	Leafhoppers, planthoppers	All adults have wings. A planthopper holds its wings tentlike over its abdomen. Leafhoppers have tapered bodies.	Piercing, sucking

Order	Some representatives	Traits	Eating style
Coleoptera	Longhorn beetles	All have hard bodies. Thick front wings cover the rear wings. A straight line runs down the back where the wings meet.	Piercing, chewing
Lepidoptera	Butterflies, moths	Wings are covered with scales.	Piercing, sucking

	Diptera	Syrphid fly (hover fly)	Adults have only one pair of wings. This fly is often mistaken for a bee. It can hover over flowers but a bee cannot.	Piercing, sucking
	Hymenoptera	Bumblebees, wasps, ants	All adults have wings. A "waist" attaches the insect's abdomen to its thorax.	Sucking, chewing

CHAPTER 8

Galls

COOPERATION AT WORK

Looking out my window, I can see an oak tree. The branches are bare of leaves because it's winter. Hundreds of small, dark, round shapes, larger than acorns but mostly smaller than golf balls, are scattered through the small twigs at the outer edges of the tree. They are galls – woody growths produced by the tree as protective homes for immature insects. You may think that the tree is very generous to house these nurseries, but the story of galls and oaks is not a story of altruism. It is a story of an ancient cooperative arrangement between plants and insects.

There are over two thousand different kinds of galls in North America, and they live on all kinds of plants. Trees such as oaks, hickories, willows, birch, and poplars are most common gall homes. In fact, there are eight hundred different kinds of galls on oak trees alone.

Galls are also common on shrubs. Rosebushes host about 125 kinds. Flowers like daisies and goldenrod claim more than 150 galls. Even algae, fungi, and lichen form galls. Galls form on all parts of a plant, though more than ninety percent form on plant leaves.

Plants are only half the story, however. The other half of the story are a special group of gall-causing insects. Cynipid wasps, from the order Hymenoptera, cause about one third of all galls. Midges cause a large number of galls as well. Aphids, sawflies, true bugs, beetles, and various moths join the ranks of lesser gall-causers. Each gall-causing insect specializes in a different kind of plant and causes a distinctive gall. An expert can examine a gall and identify the insect that caused it.

Galls are caused when an adult female insect lays its eggs on a particular part of a particular plant. Some insects lay their eggs on the surface of a plant part; others make a hole in a plant part and lay their eggs inside. The exact nature of gall formation is not yet known. It is known that insects secrete growth-regulating chemicals called auxins. In response to the auxins secreted by an egg-laying female or by the larva that develops from the egg, the plant either produces new cells or enlarges some of the existing cells. The result is a gall unique to the insect that caused it.

The inner walls of the gall are rich in proteins supplied by the plant. The developing larva can also secrete an enzyme that converts plant starch into energy-rich sugar. Species whose larval form has a jaw mechanism for chewing can tear and munch tender plant cells. Those larval species equipped with piercing or sucking mouth parts can "drink" their nourishment.

The newly developed gall protects the larva from sun, wind, rain, and predators. But this security is uncertain. Scores of small, hungry insect and

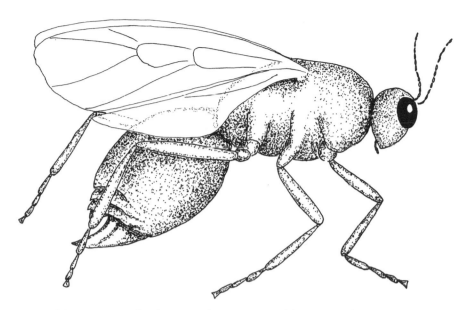

Diplolepsis rosae *(family* Cinipeds*) is just one of the many gall-causing wasps.*

mite predators hunt for an occupied gall. Some don't attack the larva but rather compete for the food available inside the gall. These competitors can cause the starvation of the larva. Other interlopers don't kill the larva but parasitize it. Sometimes even the parasites on the parasites find their way into the gall. Then there are the creatures that make the gall their home after they have eaten all the inhabitants. If the gall is big enough (some grow as large as baseballs), even small birds will move in after the mayhem has ceased.

All this traffic through a gall makes it difficult to decide which living thing formed the gall in the first place. Identifying the gall-maker is often even more difficult because many of the gall-forming insects are so small that they can't be seen by the naked eye. Through careful observation and meticulous note-keeping, scientists have discovered that each type of insect produces a distinctive gall. Galls are fingerprints that can identify the gall-maker.

Gall formation seems to be a one-sided proposition favoring the insect. The gall may, however, be a protective device for the plant; it's far better for the host plant to confine the insect invaders within the rigid walls of galls. In this way the plant prevents considerable damage that could be caused by the developing insects.

The life cycles of gall-causing insects are sometimes quite complex. For example, horned oak galls, rounded brown balls with woody spikes, form on

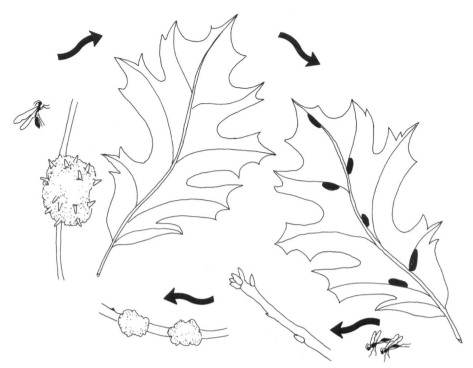

The life cycle of the horned oak gall wasp revolves around the red oak. Clockwise from left: The female wasp emerges from a horned oak gall and lays her eggs on the undersides of red oak leaves. Galls form along leaf veins. Males and females emerge and mate, and the females lay their eggs on red oak twigs. Twig galls form around the developing females.

young twigs of red oak trees. The gall-causer is the larval form of a small wasp (*Cynipid* sp.).

When female wasps lay eggs on the undersides of red oak leaves, tiny galls form along the leaf veins. The veins are the source of nutrients for the developing insect. Early in July the eggs hatch and release tiny male and female wasps. The wasps mate and the females lay their eggs on young twigs of red oaks. In this case the horned oak gall forms. It takes two years from the time the eggs are laid for the larvae to emerge as adults. The adults are all females. Horned oak galls are most easily seen during the winter when the trees are without their leaves.

All distorted and bruised leaves are not galls. Some insect larva called leaf miners live between the layers of the leaf. Recognize them by tan squiggled lines or blotches on the leaves of trees, shrubs, and wildflowers.

If you study a leaf very carefully, you will find that it has an upper and a lower skin, with additional layers inside the leaf. One of these layers is called the spongy mesophyll. Many leaf miners dwell in this spongelike middle layer and eat it. As they eat their way through the layer, the larva remove the chlorophyll-containing cells. What remains are the transparent upper and lower surfaces of the leaf. Thus we can see the tiny, flattened bodies of the leaf miners. Their flattened form is a physical adaptation to the cramped quarters where they live.

After hatching from eggs laid on the leaf, the minute larva makes a hole in the cuticle, or skin, of the leaf and crawls inside. In its snug home, the larva matures into adulthood, leaves the mine, mates, and reproduces, and the cycle begins again.

There are about 750 species of insects that cause mines. More than half that number belong to the order Lepiodoptera (moths and butterflies). The order Diptera (flies) ranks second in the number of mine-forming species. Just as different species of insects produce distinctive galls, species of leaf miners also leave their signatures in the leaves where they live. You can follow a leaf miner's mine from beginning to end by tracing it from its narrowest to its widest point.

The advantages for mine-forming larva are essentially the same as for gall-causers. Snug in their tunnels and with a ready supply of food, they are protected from the extremes of weather. But the mine is not a perfect hideaway. Some miners become food for birds, as well as wasps and other predatory insects; ripped leaves and vacant mines are telltale signs. Look for mines on the leaves of birch, elm, locust, and oak trees.

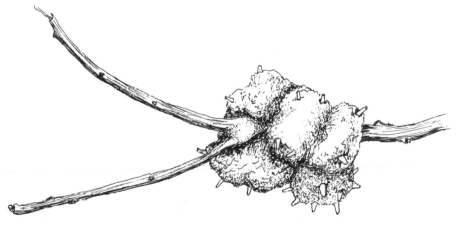

The horned oak gall protects the developing female wasp inside.

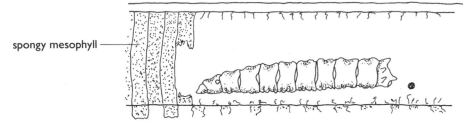

spongy mesophyll

A cross section of a leaf shows the damage caused by a developing larva.

THE WORLD OF GALLS

What to Bring	Science Skills
basic kit	*observing*
curiosity	*recording*
	inferring

OBSERVATIONS

More than ninety percent of galls form on plant leaves, but you will also find them on branches, twigs, buds, flowers, fruits, and even on roots. If you aren't sure where to begin your search for galls, start with the leaves and twigs of oak trees.

A Brief Look at Some Galls. Examine the galls you find. Are they hard, woody, succulent, or rubbery? Can you crush them with your hand? What color are they? Are they smooth, rough, bumpy, prickly, or hairy? Do they feel like velvet?

How big are they? Are all galls of the same type also the same size?

Look at their shapes. Are they round, oval, elliptical, football-shaped, or some other shape? Some galls have very queer shapes. They may look like bubbles or miniature pinecones. Some look like witches' hats. Others resemble tubes or buttons. Many are simply globs of woody material.

Assuming an insect caused the gall, can you find the exit holes the adult used to escape? How many are there? You might also find larger holes made by woodpeckers.

Galls and Food Chains. Gall insects account for an enormous amount of the protein that birds, bats, squirrels, chipmunks, mice, and other animals use for food. Can you find any evidence that animals have been chewing or gnawing on the galls?

A SAMPLE OF GALLS ON GOLDENROD STEMS

Plant #	Galls	
	shape	number
1	round	3
2	round	1
3	none	0
etc.		

EXPLORATIONS

Goldenrod and Gall Populations. Find a field with goldenrod growing in it. Examine the goldenrod for galls on its stems. Is there more than one gall on each stem? What shapes are the galls? What percentage of the goldenrods you examined have galls? Which kind of gall occurs most frequently? Is it round or egg-shaped?

Goldenrod is host to more than fifty kinds of galls. Look for tight bunches of leaves. Midges cause these galls called goldenrod bunch galls. Midges also cause raised black dots on the leaves. These are called blister galls. Galls also form on buds and flowers. Can you find any of these?

Goldenrod Elliptical Galls. One researcher suggested that exit "doors" often face north and rarely face south. He reasoned that because the north-facing side of the gall received less sunlight, it would be moist and soft. The south-facing side of the gall would become dry and hard from the greater amount of sunlight. Since the moth larva could chew its "door" more easily on the softer, north-facing side, that's where the exit would be. Look for the tiny "door" on elliptical galls. Do the doors appear more frequently on the north-facing side or on the south-facing side of the gall?

A Closer Look. The architecture inside galls is often very complex. To see some of this work you will need to open the galls. Some galls have a seam you can open with a fingernail or knife.

Observe the inside of the gall. Is there one large chamber or are there several? Make some drawings to illustrate the interior design of the more elaborate galls you find. These would be good subjects for close-up photography.

Are there any little larva or grubs inside? How many can you find? Do you see any spiders living in the gall? Are there any other critters lodging inside? How many are there and what do they look like?

A Gall Hunt. Galls are all around you. Once you begin hunting for them, you will be amazed at how easy they are to find. (See Chapter Note 2 for specifics about some galls.)

TREE GALLS

Tree	Location of gall	Appearance

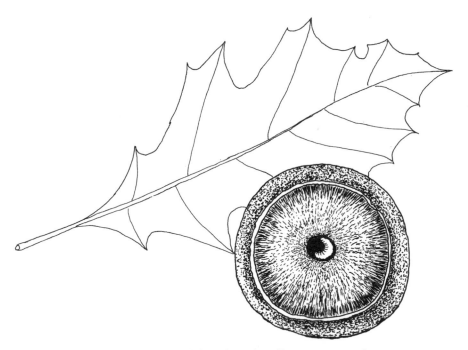

The complex internal architecture of the oak apple gall is apparent in this cross section. Note the wasp larva at the center.

The woolsower gall with its woolly filaments is caused by the gallfly Andricus seminator *and appears on white oak.*

SHRUB GALLS

Shrub	Location of gall	Appearance

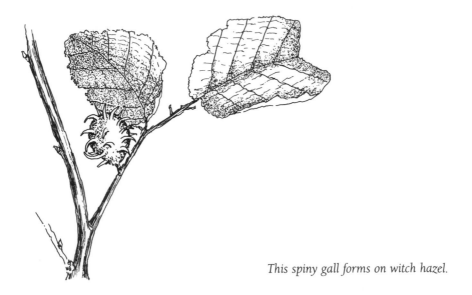

This spiny gall forms on witch hazel.

This cone gall on pussy willow is remarkably similar
to the female cones of the conifers.

WILDFLOWER GALLS

Wildflower	Location of gall	Appearance

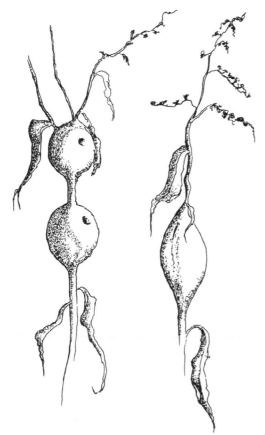

Ball and elliptical galls are commonly found on goldenrod.

A Hunt for Leaf Mines and Their Makers. On the oak trees look for leaves decorated with brown squiggles or blotches. Remove one of these leaves and hold it up to the light. Can you see the tiny larva inside? Since moths are frequent miners, the larva may be a small moth caterpillar.

You will find that some leaves have more than one mine. How many mines can you find in one leaf? Do the mines intersect with each other?

If you find a leaf that has a mine in it but you are unable to find the little caterpillar inside, look for the exit hole or slit.

Leaf Mines and Evergreens. Leaf miners aren't restricted to the leaves of broadleaf trees and shrubs. Many mines are excavated in the needles of thick-leaved pines. A telltale sign of a mine in these leaves is a yellow-tipped needle. Hold the needle up to the light. Perhaps you can see the tiny caterpillar move inside the needle.

Types of Mines. Although each species of insect makes its own type of mine, the mines can be grouped into three general types. The first is the serpentine or squiggle mine. These meandering lines make pretty designs in the leaf. The variety in patterns is almost endless.

The second type is the trumpet mine. Some people put these mines in the same group as the serpentine mines, others do not. The mine has a narrow canal at one end with a flare at the other. The flare resembles the end of a trumpet.

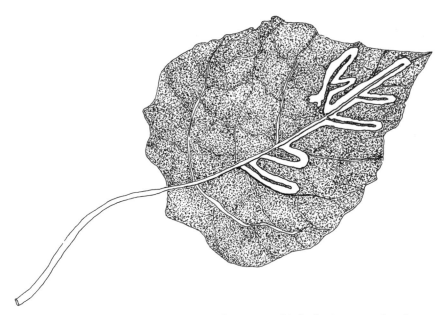

A hungry caterpillar can cause extensive damage, as this leaf mine on poplar shows.

The third kind of mine is the blotch mine. These look as though someone spilled tan paint on the leaves of a tree, shrub, or wildflower. The larva feeds in an irregular circular motion, causing blotches. Sometimes a meandering mine will end as a blotch mine.

Look for the different kinds of mines. Keep a record of the kind of plants that support leaf-mining insects and the kind of mine you find on each.

CHAPTER NOTES

1. **Gall Study.** The formal name for this branch of science is cecidology.

2. **Insects That Cause Galls.** Many insects exist in the kind of symbiotic relationship that leads to gall formation in plants. *Cecidomyia Ocellaris,* or gall midge, produces blister galls on sugar maple *(Acer saccharum.)* The fruit fly *Eurosta solidaginis* causes the round stem gall on goldenrod (*Solidago* sp.). Both of these insects belong to the order Diptera, formed from the Greek *di* = two, and *ptera* = wing.

Bees, Wasps, and Ants. Of the order Hymenoptera (*hymeno* = god of marriage, and *ptera* = wing), the gall wasp *Pontania pomum* causes the pouch gall on willows (*Salix* sp.). Another wasp, *Cynips quercusfolii,* is the architect of oak ball galls on species of oak (*Quercus* sp.).

The Aphids. *Pemphigus spirothecae* and *Pemphigus bursariusa* of the order Homoptera (*homo* = same) both cause galls to form on alder trees (*Populus* sp.), but the aphid Hormaphis hamamelidis prefers the witch hazel *(Hamamelis virginiana).*

Butterflies and Moths. The order Lepidoptera (*lepido* = scale) is also represented among those insects that cause the formation of galls in plants. *Gnorimoschema gallaesolidaginis* is a species of moth that makes its home in the species of goldenrod *Solidago canadensis.* The field guide to insects that is listed in the bibliography will provide you with more information about these and other gall-forming insects.

CHAPTER 9

Lichens

PARTNERS FOREVER

Lichens are a remarkable group of plants that can flourish in extreme climatic conditions. They thrive in Nevada's Death Valley, enduring the blazing sun of the desert day and the bitter cold of its night. Lichens have also been discovered in the forbidding polar desert of Victoria Land in the Antarctic. These tiny, tenacious plants are found in the porous Antarctica sandstone about one-tenth inch below the rock surface. They are actually growing inside the rock! Lichens grow in tropical rainforests and in the arctic tundra. But it is the cool, damp forests of the northern temperate zone that produce most of the world's lichens.

Perhaps the most basic and fascinating discovery about lichens is that each lichen is composed of two very different kinds of plants. The lichen is a green or blue-green alga and a colorless fungus living together in a very special relationship.

The exact nature of the lichen partnership remains a puzzle. One theory is that the lichen union is beneficial to each organism. In this view, the alga provides food for itself and for the fungal partner through photosynthesis. In return, the fungus supplies chemicals that accelerate food production by the alga. The tough, spongy skin of the fungus also absorbs and stores water for use by both partners. This is called the *mutualistic theory*.

A conflicting theory says that, instead of the union being mutually satisfying, the fungus is parasitic on its algal partner and often destroys some algal cells. The fungus cannot live in isolation from the alga, however. Apparently the lopsided relationship continues because the alga can produce enough cells to compensate for those destroyed by the fungus. This special symbiotic relationship is called *controlled* parasitism.

Whatever its exact nature may be, the lichen relationship did not always exist. A few million years ago algae and fungi lived independent lives. Eventually the two life forms came together to form the highly successful partnership. So far, scientists have identified about twenty thousand species of lichens.

The body of a lichen generally has four distinct layers. The top rubbery layer (upper cortex) contains a gelatinous material, which protects the lichen and helps it retain water. Beneath the cortex lies the food-producing (photosynthetic) algal layer. Fine fungal filaments called hyphae form a network within which the green algal cells are enmeshed. The hyphae can absorb and store large quantities of water, as much as three hundred times the weight of the lichen. The raw materials for photosynthesis and the food produced by the process are transported through these hairlike threads. Under the algal cells lies a relatively thick layer called the medulla. Made from loosely gathered hyphae, the medulla is a storage place for food products. A final layer, the lower

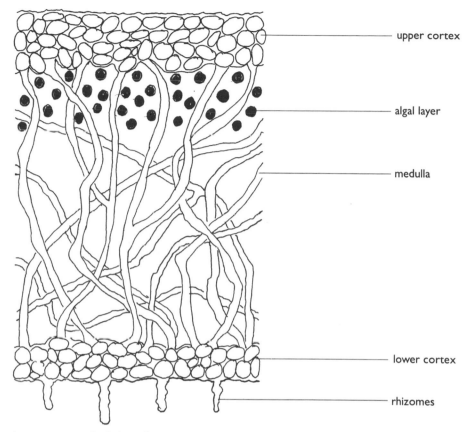

upper cortex

algal layer

medulla

lower cortex

rhizomes

A cross section of a lichen illustrates the symbiotic relationship between plant and animal. The medulla is composed of fungal filaments.

cortex, contains specialized hyphae called rhizomes that anchor the lichen to its foundation.

One of the significant contributions made by lichens is their participation in soil formation. One method is chemical in nature. When teamed with its algal partner, the fungus secrets acids. These acids etch mineral matter from the surface of rock. Some of these rock particles slough off and are carried away by wind and water. This mineral matter is an important ingredient in soil. It combines with decaying organic material to become the medium in which plants thrive.

Lichens have another method of releasing mineral particles for soil production. As the fungal fibers grow they squeeze into tiny crevices along the rock. The fibers expand and contract as they absorb and release water. This mechanical action pries away tiny particles of rock, which begin to accumulate as soil. The thin film of soil produced by these hardy pioneer plants provides a base on which other plants, such as mosses, can get a foothold. Soil-making is a slow process, but lichens may live several hundred years.

Another service lichens provide is nitrogen fixation. All living things need nitrogen to build proteins. But although nitrogen makes up seventy-eight percent of the air we breathe, animals and most plants cannot use nitrogen in its gaseous form. Happily for us, and for many other life forms, many lichens have a blue-green alga as one of the partners. In addition to chlorophyll, these specialized algae have accessory pigments that can grab nitrogen from the air and "fix" it into new organic compounds. Through the process of decay, the nitrogen in the lichen becomes available to other plants.

Lichens serve other functions in nature. They are the major food supply for reindeer and caribou in the arctic tundra. They supplement the diets of deer, elk, moose, and grouse in lower latitudes. Many birds, including hummingbirds, the wood pewee, and the gray plover, use lichens as nesting materials.

Human beings have also found uses for lichens. The dyeing properties of lichens have been known for a long time; the colors in Harris tweeds and Madras shirts come from lichen pigments. The manufacturing of some antibiotics utilizes lichen products. The perfume industry has been using lichen products as fixative agents for a very long time.

Lichens may seem to be unimportant, but they are far more valuable than their appearance suggests. These primitive plants are important to ecological systems in a very special way. They are extremely sensitive to man-made pollution. When lichens are killed by air pollutants, as they have been in many parts of the world, we know that other living organisms are also in danger. Lichens issue an early warning when there is danger in the air we breathe. We should listen.

THE WORLD OF LICHENS

What to Bring
basic kit
stiff plastic
camera and macro lens
pocket knife
chalk
baggie
oil-based paint
hand compass
perseverance

Science Skills
observing
measuring
recording
classifying

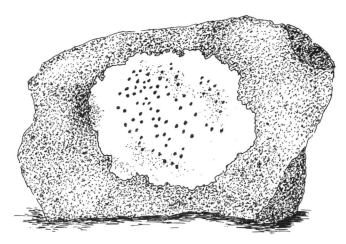

Pitted lichen (Lecanora calcarea) *is a crusty lichen that grows on limestone. The upper surface of its thin whitish body (thallus) is marked with numerous small black fruiting bodies.*

OBSERVATIONS

In the activities that follow, you may discover some interesting things about lichens and how they live. Should you want to dig a little deeper into their world, the books listed in the bibliography are among the best in the field. Lichenology is one of the few areas of study where an amateur can make significant contributions. If you like lichens, go to it!

Types of Lichens and Where to Find Them. The bodies of lichens come in a variety of forms, and it is the fungal partner that determines the shape. For convenience, lichenologists have assigned lichens to one of three categories based on their shape: crusty (crustose), ruffled or leaflike (foliose), and shrublike, hairlike, or strap-shaped (fruticose). Learning which lichen belongs to what group is your first challenge.

Crustose lichens are the most primitive. Look for them growing in thin, flat mats on rocks or cement, where they look like gray-white, yellow-orange, greenish, or even brilliant red splashes of paint. You'll find them on rocky outcrops in old fields and on mountain trails, as well as on headstones and old buildings. Because these lichens are difficult to remove from the rocks that support them, it may seem that the lichens are growing out of the rocks rather than on them. A few types of lichens do have fine filaments growing nearly half an inch into the rock face.

Crustose lichens range from pinhead size to several inches in diameter. You also will see large patches where many smaller blotches have grown together.

Shield lichen (Parmelia aurulenta) *is a grayish green leafy lichen found on northern trees and logs. It is one of the most commonly collected Parmelias.*

Foliose lichens are those most often seen and recognized as lichens. These lichens have a leaflike body that is often crinkly and divided into lobes or branches. They seem to curl away from their foundation. Leafy lichens frequently resemble lace doilies, and they come in a variety of colors. They can be gray-green, brown, or slate gray, and some will turn bright green if you wet them. Unlike the crusty lichens, leafy lichens are attached to their foundations only here and there by a system of tiny threads called rhizomes. Look for foliose lichens on tree trunks or on dead branches and twigs strewn in the litter of a woodland floor. The common dog lichen (*Peltigera canina*) is a foliose lichen. Its color ranges from blue-gray to brown and it has toothlike fruiting bodies along its wavy edges. The surface of this lichen is furry. Use your magnifier to see the tiny hairs. Other foliose lichens include the genera *Parmelia*, *Lobaria*, *Physcia*, *Cetraria*, and *Sticta*.

Fruticose lichens can either be upright or hang gracefully from tree branches. One type of hanging lichen is old-man's-beard. This lichen belongs to the genus *Usnea*. (See Chapter Note 1 for a look-alike.) It hangs from the

The red caps (fruiting bodies) of the shrubby lichen British soldier (Cladonia cristatella) *sit on greenish gray branching stalks. Look for them on humus and rotting logs.*

trees as a tangle of whitish- or yellow-gray threads. Lichen in this genus are found in spruce-fir forests along the coast of Maine, rocky outcrops in Georgian Bay, the forests of the Pacific Northwest, and in other coniferous forests of the northern temperate zone.

Another type of fruticose lichen, belonging to the genus *Cladonia*, is British soldier. The tiny, red hats sitting on the top of stalks are reproductive centers. These lichens are striking when set off by a light dusting of snow. Look for them on old fence posts and on pieces of rotting wood. My split-rail fence is dotted with a healthy population of British soldiers that has been increasing for several years. Most fruticose lichens are either *Usnea* sp. or *Cladonia* sp.

Additional Lichen Hangouts. Although they can endure harsh weather, lichens cannot cope with serious air pollution problems from sulfur compounds, carbon monoxide, or other impurities. Most lichens are unable to excrete the pollutants they absorb during metabolism. The buildup of these pollutants ultimately kills them. For this reason, keeping detailed records of changes in lichen populations is one method for determining air quality in a region. Some highly resistant types, such as *Cladonia*, are able to live in a polluted environment and are not useful as pollution indicators.

Don't look for lichens in urban areas. Mountainous areas where the air is

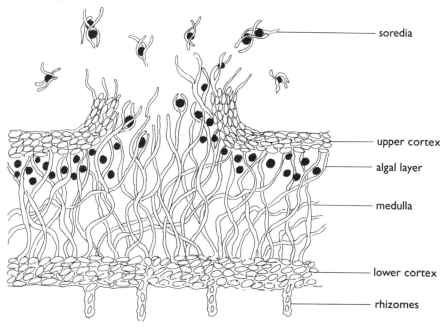

soredia

upper cortex

algal layer

medulla

lower cortex

rhizomes

In lichen reproduction, algal cells surrounded by hyphae (soredia) are released from the lichen to drift away on wind currents.

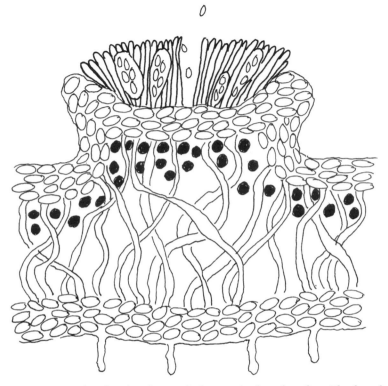

Lichen spores are produced within fruiting bodies on the fungal surface. The fungal filaments that grow from these spores will develop into a lichen only if they encounter a suitable algae.

clean, deserts of the southwest, and the coniferous forests of the northern-temperate zone are places you can expect to find lichens. The cleaner the air, the greater the variety of lichens.

How to Look for Lichens. Go on a neighborhood walk. Look on stone walls, wooden fences, and concrete buildings. Don't forget to take your notebook; keep a record of what you find. If you enjoy lichen-watching and continue to do it for a long time, you may discover patterns, changes, or trends in lichen populations.

On what is the lichen growing? With the help of your compass, determine the direction the lichen is facing. Is it growing on the north, south, east, or west side of a stone wall, rocky outcrop, or tree? What color is it? To what group (crustose, foliose, or fruticose) does it belong?

With the help of your hand lens, examine the bodies of the lichens. You may find some curious black dots scattered over the surface. These are probably reproductive structures. Do you find them on all types of lichens? Do they appear throughout the year, or are they present only during certain months?

Examine different types of foliose lichens. Is the color on the underside of the lobes the same or different from the upper surface? Is the color uniform on the surface and along the edges? Are there hairlike projections growing out of any portion of the lichen? Do you see toothlike projections along the leafy edges? In the dog lichen these are reproductive structures.

EXPLORATIONS

Is It a Lichen or a Fungus? Lichens growing on tree trunks are often confused with fungi that also prefer this habitat. With your pocket knife, chip off a piece of lichen and the bark that holds it.

Are the anchoring threads attached to the bark, or are the filaments growing through the bark? Is there a mass of cottonlike material on the underside of the bark? (See Chapter Note 2 for fungal facts.) Lichens generally do not harm the tree. Some fungi are parasitic, however, and can damage the tree. (See Chapter 14 on fungi.)

Lichen Layers. Lichen bodies are made of several layers. One of those layers contains green or blue-green algal cells held by fungal filaments. Cut across the lichen body as in the illustration. With a hand lens, look for the layers.

What is the color of the cortex, or skin, of your lichen? Look for the green algal layer, the white medulla that contains white fungal threads, and the lower surface or cortex.

The exercises that follow require patience, perseverance, and love. They are not for those who need to hurry. Lichens do not know speed.

Lichen Locations. Find a tree with lichens growing on its bark. Draw chalk lines around the tree trunk about one foot above and one foot below chest height. The band you have made should be about two feet wide.

Examine the lichens that are inside the band. Look for crustose, foliose, and fruticose lichens. Does there seem to be only one kind of lichen on the tree trunk, or are there examples of each type?

With your compass, determine which portions of the tree are facing north, south, east, and west and mark them. Count the number of lichens in each section. Where are the greatest numbers of lichens?

Is any portion of your band shaded throughout the day? How does this seem to affect the number and type of lichens growing on that part of the tree?

Try a similar exploration to learn about the lichens that grow on rocks. What differences did you discover?

Growth Rate in Lichens. Lichens grow very slowly. Certain lichens grow slowly when they are young, but as they mature their growth rate increases.

Find some lichens growing in an area that is easy for you to visit. With an 8½- by 11-inch piece of flexible transparent plastic, cover the lichens with the plastic and secure it with some tape. Using a permanent marker such as oil-based paint, draw the four corners of the plastic on the lichen foundation. You now have a reference point to use when you return to take measurements of lichen growth.

Lay the plastic sheet over the lichen you are studying. With a fine, felt-tipped pen, trace its outline onto the plastic sheet. Record on your plastic sheet the date of your tracing and the precise location of the lichen. When you return to the site at a future date, you can make another tracing of the same lichen by simply slipping your plastic sheet into the corners you made with the paint.

How much did the lichens grow over a summer, in a year, or in several years? Did they grow evenly around a central point or did one portion grow more than another? Describe the growth pattern. If you observe your lichens for a few months, you may find evidence of nibblers. (See Chapter Note 3 for some published growth measurements.)

Find several lichens of the same type growing in different locations and repeat the steps. What was the average rate of growth for that type of lichen?

You can extend this activity to include several different types of lichens. Compare the growth rates. Compare the growth patterns. Are they similar or different?

A Lichen Portfolio. Make a photographic record of the lichens you find. A 35-mm camera with a macro lens for close-ups should work well. You might need a flash attachment if you are working in the dim light of a spruce-fir forest.

Be sure to record the date you took the pictures, the location of each lichen, the type of foundation, and whether the lichen was wet or dry (color is sometimes altered by moisture).

CHAPTER NOTES

I. **Lichen Look-Alike.** The lichen old-man's beard of the genus *Usnea* is often confused with a flowering plant called Spanish moss. You can find Spanish moss hanging from southern trees, such as live oak. It also graces the branches of other plants. Spanish moss is not a parasite, so it doesn't do any harm as it dangles from other kinds of vegetation.

2. Fungus Facts. To distinguish absolutely between a lichen and a fungus requires microscopic examination, but there is a general guideline you can use in the field. With the aid of your hand lens, gently lift a lobe of the lichen from the tree bark. If the anchoring threads are *on* the bark and not coming *through* it, then you are probably observing a lichen. The threads of a fungal mat will grow through the bark and will appear as a white mass on the undersurface of the bark.

Except for a few uncommon species, lichens are not parasitic on trees. But fungal growth, such as the common bracket and turkey tail fungi, remove nutrients from the tree for their own use. The tree will eventually succumb. Some bracket fungi and turkey tails get their nutrients from dead material. Thus, some of the fungi on dead trees may not have caused their death.

3. Growth measurements. These growth measurements for some of the more common lichens are taken from *The Biology of Lichens* by Mason Hale.

Lichen	Average Annual Radial Rate (mm)
Foliose	
Peltigera canina	3.0 mm–7.0 mm
Fruticose	
Cladonis alpestris	3.4 mm
Crustose	
Diploschistes sp.	2.0 mm

CHAPTER 10

Vines

SEEKING A PLACE IN THE SUN

A soft wall of morning glories grew in profusion against the wooden shingles of my childhood home. Those vines, twined around the lattice work, seemed to be reaching out in a deliberate quest to reach higher and higher. The wisteria that claimed the doorway of a friend's house also fascinated me. Stout and woody, its stems draped over the curved trellis. Bunches of sweet-smelling, lavender flowers dangled from it like clusters of berries. Both of these vines left me wondering: Why do vines climb and how do they do it?

Where plants have enough water, soil, and mild temperatures, there is keen competition among them for sunlight. Trees compete by spreading their leaves over a large, three-dimensional space above their strong, woody stems. The construction of these stems, however, is slow and uses lots of energy and raw materials.

Vines compete for sunlight using a different strategy. Their woody stems are lighter, more flexible, and strong without being rigid. This gives the vine the advantage of fast growth. This rapid growth enables some vines to reach open spaces on the ground where they can spread their leaves over large areas.

Virginia creeper is one of these sprawling vines. You can find it in your backyard, in parks, and in vacant lots. It grows well in the shade of trees and shrubs, as well as in open spaces. Its creeping strategy has brought it success from Maine to Florida to Texas to the Rocky Mountains.

But the creeping behavior of vines is not an adequate solution where there is no direct sunlight at ground level. Vines need alternate strategies. Virginia creeper and other trailing vines not only worm their way along the ground, they also crawl up supporting structures such as nearby trees, stone walls, houses, or fences.

Often sun-loving vines grow upward at heavy cost to the trees that support them. The vines in a tree may become so extensive and heavy that they stunt the tree's growth or even topple the entire system to the ground. Some years ago vines spreading through Oklahoma overwhelmed a great many elm and hackberry trees. Scientists removed samples of wood from dead trees and examined the growth rings. The study revealed that the trees grew very little during their last years.

Vines cling tenaciously to their living supports. You may know from experience that vines have some slick tricks for climbing. Scientists who study vines group them according to climbing strategies identified long ago by Charles Darwin in his pioneering study of vines, *The Movements and Habits of Climbing Plants.*

adhesive disks
on a tendril

Virginia creeper (Parthenocissus quinquefolia) *employs adhesive disks to attach itself to support structures.*

Scientists have identified five basic climbing methods of vines: leaning or trailing, weaving, rooting, grasping, and sticking. Vines that employ the leaning strategy just flop over plants and other objects. Some vines simply drape themselves over whatever support is available. Other vines, like rambler roses, have thorns to keep their stems from slipping off the supporting structures.

Weaving vines grow in and out of structures such as bushes, chainlink fences, trellises, or other suitable objects.

Some vines climb up tree trunks or stone walls using tiny roots called adventitious roots that, at various points, grow from their stems. Poison ivy climbs this way. Consequently, it is classified as a rooting vine. Such a vine anchors its roots in cracks and fissures in whatever will support it. English ivy attaches itself to walls in this way.

There are several kinds of grasping vines. Some grow straight up and others follow a spiral path in which the whole stem encircles the support. The leading tip of this type of vine is sensitive to touch, it guides the vine around any convenient vertical support. Some of these vines twine clockwise and others twine counterclockwise. Honeysuckle twines clockwise, but Morning glories are famous for their counterclockwise twining. Most twining vines don't seem to have a preference. With other grasping vines, only part of the vine encircles the support. They produce delicate tendrils from their stems, leaves,

Trumpet vine (Campsis radicans) *employs aerial rootlets (adventitious roots) that emerge from its woody stem to anchor itself to a suitable support.*

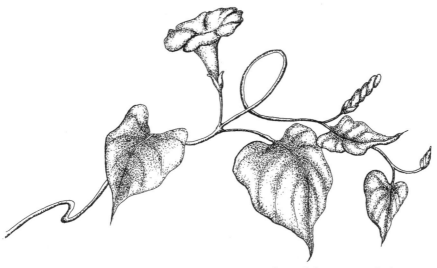

Morning glory (Ipomoea purpurea) *is a grasping vine that exhibits counterclockwise twining.*

| adventitious roots | tendrils | twining | touch-sensitive leaves |

Vines use specific climbing strategies to reach sunlight.

leaf stalks, or flowers. The tendrils grow outward until they find something substantial to grasp. Contact with a suitable object signals the tendril to twine around the object. Some tendrils start coiling around the support in a few seconds. Grapes use tendrils to climb.

Sometimes, as in the case of Virginia creeper, the tendrils develop adhesive disks. These disks permit the vine to attach itself to a support. Virginia creeper

Bittersweet (Celastrus sp.) is a woody twining vine.

Honeysuckle (Lonicera sp.) is a climbing shrub that produces a berrylike fruit.

and other vines that use this strategy are the sticking vines. The small adhesive disks are found at the ends of tendrils, branches, or rootlets. They produce a sticky resinous material that the vine uses to glue itself to rough surfaces, such as tree trunks and stone walls.

Some vines can switch climbing methods. If conditions change, Boston ivies can switch from sticking to weaving, and grapes can switch from clinging to gluing.

Darwin considered these climbing methods to indicate progression along the evolutionary ladder. He considered rootlets the most primitive of climbing techniques and adhesive disks the most advanced. You will find examples of each kind of climber when you begin to look more closely at vines.

THE WORLD OF VINES

What to Bring
basic kit
camera
spring scale
string
tape

Science Skills
observing
measuring

OBSERVATIONS

Vines come in a variety of sizes and shapes. You will find them growing on trees, shrubs, and bushes in backyards, parks, and schoolyards. They climb up buildings and telephone poles. You may even find an old house or barn covered by a blanket of vines. Look for vines at the woodland-field border where grasses, weeds, vines, and shrubs battle for dominance.

You can easily identify many vines. Virginia creeper (*Parthenocissus* sp.), grape (*Vitis* sp.), wisteria (*Wisteria* sp.), bittersweet (*Celastrus* sp.), trumpet vine (*Campsis radicans*), greenbrier (*Smilax* sp.), poison ivy (*Rhus radicans*), and honeysuckle (*Lonicera* sp.) are easily found. For making other vine identifications, use the field guide by George W. D. Symonds listed in the bibliography.

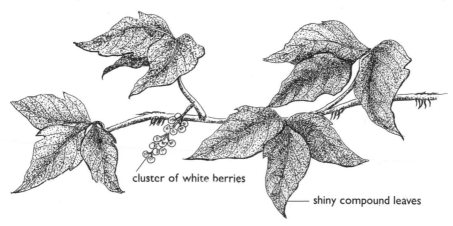

cluster of white berries

shiny compound leaves

Poison ivy (Rhus radicans) can be identified by its characteristic compound leaves and clusters of white, waxy fruit.

CLIMBING METHODS AND VINES

Method	Vine
A. Leaning	
1. without thorns	
2. with thorns	
B. Weaving	
C. Rooting	
D. Grasping	
1. twining	
a. clockwise	
b. counterclockwise	
2. clinging	
a. tendrils on stem	
b. tendrils on leaves	
c. tendrils on leaf stems	
E. Sticking	
1. disks on tendrils	
2. disks on branchlets	

You can use this table to check off the varieties of climbing vines you encounter. Include a description of each vine to help later in vine identification.

Growth Patterns of Vine Leaves. Leaf arrangement patterns, along with other characteristics, are used to identify the vine. Are the leaves growing opposite each other? Are they growing alternately like steps along the stem? (Look for leaf arrangements in Chapter 1.)

Leaves can be simple or compound. A leaf is simple if a single leaf blade is attached to the stem by the petiole (the leaf stem that attaches the leaf blade to the twig or stem). Compound leaves have more than one leaf blade attached to a petiole.

Are the leaves simple or are they compound? Are the compound leaves shaped like the palm of your hand (palmate) as in Virginia creeper? Be careful! The leaves of poison ivy are palmately compound in groups of three. Remember the warning "leaves of three, let it be." (See Chapter Note, on poison ivy.)

A Seed Collection. Autumn is a good time to look for seeds. You will

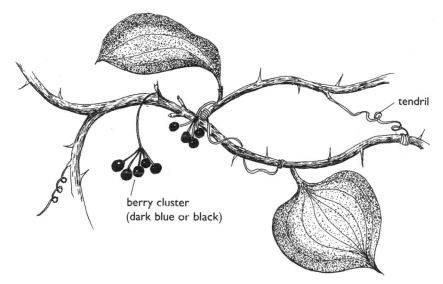

Greenbrier (Smilax rotundifolia) *is a high-climbing woody vine.*

discover that some seeds are contained within berries, while others are inside pods. Look for the various seed containers developed by vines. Keep a record of what you find on the chart below.

A Twining Experiment. Find a vine that twines up a vertical support. Invent a way to determine if the vine will continue to twine if the support is placed in a horizontal position?

VINES AND THEIR SEED CONTAINERS

Vine	Containers	
	pods	berries
greenbrier		
Dutchman's pipe		
wisteria		
bittersweet		
Virginia creeper		
grape		
trumpet vine		
honeysuckle		

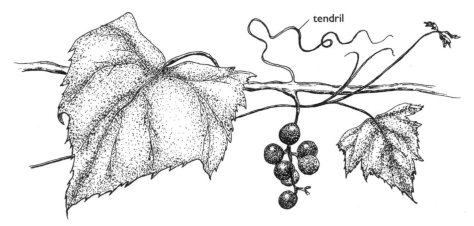

Wild grape (Vitis labrusca) *utilizes tendrils for climbing.*

Touchy Tendrils. Find a vine that uses tendrils to climb. Locate a tendril that is not wrapped around a support. Stroke one side of the tendril very gently with the point of a pencil. What happens and how long does it take? Examine several other kinds of vines that produce tendrils. Do the tendrils on these vines respond to touch in the same way?

Tendrils with Attachment Disks. Examine the tendrils of Boston ivy or English ivy. How many disks grow from each tendril? What do the disks look like? Can you pull them off the wall easily? On what kind of surfaces do you find them growing? Wood? Concrete? Brick? Smooth or rough?

Find the attachment disks of Virginia creeper. Describe the tendrils that are not attached to some object. What color are they? How big are they? What happens to the tendrils after they have become attached to a support? What color are the tendrils that are already in place on a support? Are they straight or twisted?

Compare the tendrils and the disks of an older part of the vine with that of the younger portion. What do you notice?

How Strong Is Strong? It's been said that the attachment disks of Virginia creeper can require more than five pounds of force to remove them from a point of attachment. Find a spring scale, like that in fishing to weigh the catch. Attach one end of a string to the scale and the other end to a tendril. You can use some tape to secure the string to the tendril. How much force is required to pull the disk away from the surface where it was attached? Try this with other disk-attached vines, such as Boston ivy and English ivy.

CHAPTER NOTE

Poison ivy *(Rhus radicans)*. This vine is often confused with other vines with compound leaves. Many people are allergic to the oil (urushiol) that is secreted by the leaves, stems, roots, flowers, and berries of poison ivy. Inhalation of smoke from burning poison ivy is extremely dangerous.

There are many plants with compound leaves that are perfectly safe to touch. Staghorn sumac, Virginia creeper, blackberry, and young saplings of box elder are often confused with poison ivy. If you are unsure about the safety of a particular plant, use a field guide to identify the plant.

PART III
THE FOREST FLOOR

N ow we get right down to ground level to investigate the surface litter, a forgotten habitat thriving beneath our feet. We seldom think about this ecosystem because many of the life forms found there are so tiny that they can be seen only with a microscope. Bacteria and microfungi are the most important inhabitants of this dark world. They are the decomposers that recirculate nutrients through the system. Other inhabitants of the surface layer of soil, such as the eight-legged mite, are as minute as a grain of sand. Springtails and snow fleas are larger members of this community. The moist world of the surface litter is ideal for larger creatures such as millipedes and earthworms. These invertebrates are also part of the decomposition team.

This thriving community is not unique to the forest floor. You can find these creatures at work just beyond your back door, wherever organic material accumulates. In this section of the book you will learn more about ants, spiders, and other organisms that live just beneath your feet.

CHAPTER 11

Chipmunks

WINNERS AT THE GAME OF LIFE

Chipmunks are a species unique to the New World. Their lineage can be traced to the now-extinct first squirrel (*Protosciurus*), which appeared during the Oligocene some forty million years ago. Our present-day marmots (groundhogs), antelope squirrels, ground squirrels, prairie dogs, red squirrels, tree squirrels, flying squirrels, and chipmunks all evolved from that prototype.

Eventually the chipmunk gang separated and formed two groups. One of these groups is the eastern chipmunk (*Tamias striatus*) and the other group includes three species: the least chipmunk (*Eutamias minimus*), the yellow-pine chipmunk (*E. amoenus*), and the Townsend chipmunk (*E. townsendii*).

Except during the breeding season, chipmunks don't interact much with each other. You may occasionally see these woodland imps squabble over territorial rights or positions in the social hierarchy. Although there is often a lot of squealing and rolling on the ground, none of the combatants ever get seriously injured.

In March or April chipmunks emerge from their burrows and begin their mating ritual. After a thirty-one-day gestation period, females give birth to a litter of two to eight tiny, hairless, and completely dependent pups. The adult females care for the young without any help from the males. Male chipmunks do not take part in any aspect of housekeeping or raising of the young. Neither are they committed to one female.

Chipmunks have remarkable cheek pouches extending down along each side of their necks. These pouches can hold impressive numbers of seeds. One investigator counted 3,700 blueberry seeds in the pouches of one chipmunk. Another tallied ninety-three ragweed seeds in the cheek pouches of another chipmunk. These expandable cheek pouches allow chipmunks to reduce the number of excursions they make between the food source and the safety of the burrow.

Although you might think chipmunks fill their pouches to capacity, a wise chipmunk is more moderate. An overstuffed chipmunk might not be able to fit its head through the burrow opening, which is generally no larger than two inches in diameter. The inability to run at top speed because of too much cargo is a serious problem for chipmunks being pursued by predators.

By November the autumn nut-gathering ceases. Chipmunks enter their nests, where they remain until March. During this time chipmunks alternate between sleep and wakefulness. The sleep of the chipmunk lasts three to seven days. While sleeping, the chipmunk's metabolic rate is only fifteen percent of the normal rate. Chipmunks don't store body fat in the way that woodchucks

With both cheek pouches full, a foraging chipmunk can carry as much as two tablespoons of flower and grass seeds.

and other hibernating animals do; when they awake they restore their energy reserves by feeding on their cache of nuts and seeds. You might see chipmunks aboveground for short periods of time resting in the sun on a mild winter day. They don't wander very far from their burrows, though; predators are especially hungry in winter.

Scientists who study the place of chipmunks in the ecology of the forest have discovered that they are not a major component of the diet of larger mammals. They are an alternative food source for fox, coyote, mink, raccoon, red squirrel, and some predatory birds when their preferred foods are in scant supply. Thus, chipmunks serve as a buffer species.

A chipmunk burrow extends about three feet underground. New burrows are simple. They have an entrance, a tunnel, and a sleeping chamber. Since chipmunks generally use the same burrows year after year, however, they regularly do extensive remodeling. The burrows of older chipmunks are a labyrinth of tunnels with several chambers. The sleeping chamber doubles as a pantry, since chipmunks store their food under their mattresses of dried leaves and forest litter. It may also be used as a birthing room and nursery. Because they are fastidious animals, a remaining room serves as a toilet.

The chipmunk's burrow-building is an engineering feat. There is usually little evidence aboveground that digging is in progress. The first job is construction of a work tunnel, which the tiny builder carves out with its feet and nose. The rooms and an entrance hole get scooped out from inside the work

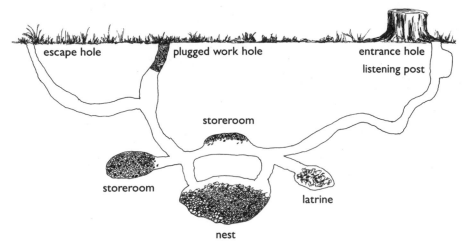

Chipmunks construct extensive burrows with several entrances.

tunnel. Dirt and other debris are later used to fill the work tunnel. Usually hidden by a cover of stones, tree bark, or a small piece of sod, the entrance hole is not easy to find. If you are very quiet during the spring, you may see a small disk of earth pushed aside, followed by an impish head peering over the edge.

THE WORLD OF CHIPMUNKS

What to Bring	Science Skills
binoculars	*observing*
watch with second hand	*recording*

OBSERVATIONS

You can find the eastern chipmunk *(Tamias striatus)* as easily in wooded urban parks as you can in a forest. They are common visitors to campsites where they can get a friendly handout. Listen to them scamper in the woodland underbrush. In areas with enough trees and food you can even find their nests in abandoned buildings.

The smallest chipmunk in North America is the least chipmunk *(Eutamias minimus)*. Look for them at the forest's edge or in second-growth areas that have been timbered or burned. Chipmunks also live in the alpine tundra.

The yellow-pine chipmunks *(Eutamias amoenus)* prefer high altitudes within their range, but they can be found in grassy valleys. They like areas covered by low shrubs. Because of their remote habitat, they don't have much contact with people. But they won't turn down an offer of sunflower seeds from a friendly wilderness camper.

Unlike other chipmunks, Townsend chipmunks *(Eutamias townsendii)* prefer coastal regions within their west coast range. It's not unusual to find them on timber-studded beaches and in the ferny underbrush of coastal forests.

Chipmunks are diurnal animals. They are most active in the early morning hours and in the late afternoon. They are especially active on warm, sunny, windless days.

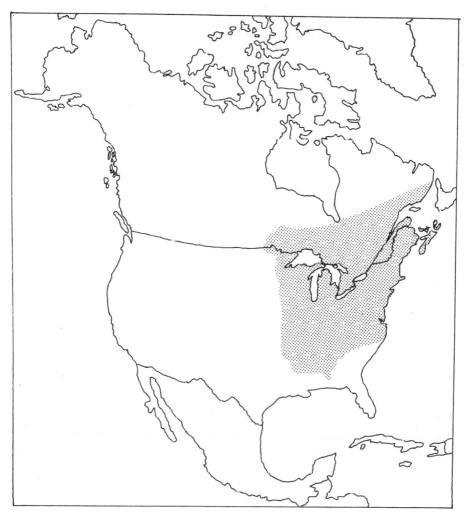

The range of the eastern chipmunk (Tamias striatus) *is extensive.*

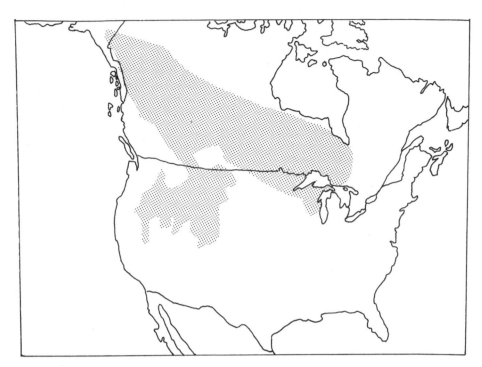

The least chipmunk (Eutamias minimus) *is found mostly in Canada and the Northwest.*

A Close Look at Chipmunks. You can make some interesting observations about the habitat and life-style of chipmunks as they scurry by. What color is the chipmunk? Is it brown, rusty, cinnamon, yellow-brown, or some other colors? What color are its stripes? How many are there? How are they arranged? The answers to these questions will vary with the species you observe.

Is the chipmunk's back the same color as its belly? What does this color pattern tell you about the life of the chipmunk? (See Chapter Note 1, on shades of color.)

How long is its tail relative to its body? Compare this length to the relative length of the gray squirrel's tail. What differences in their life-styles might account for the difference in tail length? (See Chapter Note 2, on tails.)

Chipmunk Movements. Watch the path a chipmunk follows as it moves from one place to another. Is it a simple nonstop run, or is it marked by a series of starts and stops?

Chipmunks often "freeze" when they think danger is near, and they can remain frozen for a long time. How long do the freezes last? Can you cause them to happen?

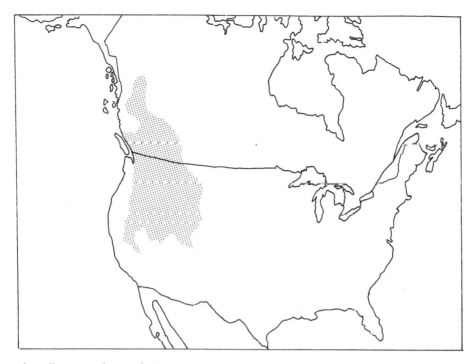

The yellow-pine chipmunk (Eutamias amoenus) *prefers the alpine environment of the Northwest and Canada.*

The Townsend chipmunk (Eutamius townsendii) *is found only in the Pacific Northwest and parts of British Columbia.*

A chipmunk's stripes are effective camouflage on the forest floor.

EXPLORATIONS

The Eyes and Ears of Chipmunks. Chipmunk eyes are placed on the side of its head. This provides the animal with a visual field of ninety degrees on each side. Chipmunks can detect motion very well and are especially good at observing shadows cast by flying objects, which could be hawks or owls.

Compared to squirrels, chipmunks don't have a good sense of smell. Their ears, however, are superb instruments for picking up sounds. Toss a peanut on the ground near a chipmunk. How does it find the nut? Can the chipmunk find it as easily if you toss it farther away?

Chipmunk Behaviors. Chipmunks display a wide range of behaviors. Below is a description of some behaviors and their labels. A detailed list of behaviors appears in Dr. Lawrence Wishner's book (see bibliography).

If the chipmunk is sitting with its front paws on ground and its back straight, it is *alert*. If its body is flat on the ground and its back is arched, the chipmunk is *frozen*. If a chipmunk is standing upright with its back straight and paws not clasped, it is in the *duckpin* position.

When loosely coiled or on the ground, the tail is *relaxed*. When held upright, it is in *alarm* position.

Food Gathering and Preferences. Investigators have discovered that chipmunks will gather as many nuts as they can find, even when their stores are well stocked. Watch as a chipmunk gathers nuts. How many does it put in its pouches?

What types of food do chipmunks seem to prefer? On the ground, place a variety of nuts, such as hazelnuts, almonds, hickories, and acorns from white oaks. Which do they eat? Offer other foods, such as blueberries, strawberries, and orange slices. Does the chipmunk eat these? (See Chapter Note 3, on food.)

Pathways to Burrows. During fall foraging and spring mating chipmunks are very active, so you might be able to find a chipmunk burrow. Watch the chipmunks that enter and leave the burrow.

Are there any distinctive behaviors or markings on the chipmunk that help you to distinguish them from each other? A scar on its ear or on its shoulder? A tattered tail? Is there a behavior that's unique to a particular chipmunk?

Watch a chipmunk as it goes off to find some food. How long did it take the chipmunk to return? Does it follow the same path back to the burrow each time, or does it make new paths? Does the path follow a straight line? What happens if you put an obstacle, such as a row of small rocks, across the path? (See Chapter Note 4, on trails.)

Early Morning Activity. You'll have to be up early to find out what a chipmunk does first thing in the morning. At what time did the chipmunk first appear? Did it first poke its nose out of the burrow and look around, or did it emerge all the way? What did it do when it came out?

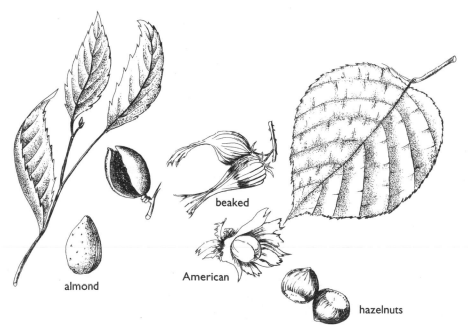

beaked

American

almond

hazelnuts

Chipmunks subsist on a variety of nuts and seeds.

Chipmunks are known for their personal hygiene. Observe chipmunks grooming. Because mites and fleas are often problems, chipmunks frequently take dust baths to remove bugs and excess oil from their fur. Observe a dust bath. (See Chapter Note 5, on grooming.)

Chipmunk Songs. One song chipmunks sing is a high-pitched *chip*, which they often repeat for an extended period of time. What is the longest time you hear them sing that song?

Another sound chipmunks make is a combination of a *chip* followed by a trill. It is usually sung after danger has passed. Listen for it.

A third sound is a soft, low-pitched, clucking sound. Chipmunks are good ventriloquists, so it may be difficult to find the source of the sounds.

CHAPTER NOTES

1. **Shades of Color.** Chipmunks climb trees to escape from predators and to find food. Their bodies are camouflaged so that the light color on the underside makes it difficult for a predator looking up the tree to see its prey. From above, the striped back of the chipmunk is equally difficult to see.

2. **Chipmunk Tails.** Chipmunks do not need bushy tails. The squirrel uses its tail for balance as it runs in the trees and along telephone wires and fences. A bushy tail on a chipmunk, which spends most of its time in a burrow or foraging on the ground, would be a liability because it would pick up woodland litter and soil.

3. **Chipmunk Food.** Chipmunks enjoy a variety of foods besides seeds and nuts. They sometimes eat mushrooms and other fungi. Perennial bulbs will do if they are easily available. Moles, grasshoppers, small frogs, salamanders, and small bird eggs have been known to satisfy chipmunk hunger. Chipmunks find water trapped in fallen leaves and in small pools on the ground. In the breeding season chipmunks drink as much as 25 percent of their body weight.

4. **Chipmunk Trails.** Chipmunks tend to follow the same path from food source to burrow. The path doesn't follow a straight line but twists through the underbrush.

5. **Chipmunk Grooming.** A chipmunk grooms its face and head first, followed by a cleanup of chest, belly, back, and thighs. It usually grooms its tail last, so rapidly you have to be alert to see it. The chipmunk first places the base of its tail in the space between its molars and incisors. Then, with a graceful sweep, the chipmunk pulls its tail through the space, washing it with its saliva.

This careful attention to grooming is probably a defense against predators that rely on scent to find their prey.

Chipmunks are also prey of the botfly, which burrows under the skin and deposits its eggs. The larva leave after hatching, but the site may become infected. Frequent grooming helps with this problem.

CHAPTER 12

Spiders

NO NEED FOR FEAR

These eight-legged creatures generate all kinds of irrational behavior in otherwise rational people. Why? Perhaps because people think spiders are hairy and ugly. They are active at night, so people associate them with skeletons, bats, and witches. Many people believe that spiders are poisonous. A sneaky spider gets blamed for any strange bite or swelling. But do spiders deserve their bad reputation? In this chapter, we'll decide for ourselves.

Spiders belong to a group called arthropods. Arthropods are animals that have jointed appendages and a hard external covering or skeleton that protects their internal body parts. The large phyllum Arthropoda contains about eighty percent of all living creatures. The animals in it belong to one of three classes: crustaceans, insects, or arachnids. Spiders are in the arachnid group, along with harvestmen, ticks, mites, and scorpions.

Although often mistaken for insects, spiders differ from them in several ways. For example, the insect body is divided into three sections: head, chest (thorax), and abdomen. The spider body has only two divisions: cephalothorax (fused head and chest) and abdomen. The insect thorax is three-parted, and each part has a pair of jointed walking legs. In contrast, a spider moves about on four pairs of jointed legs attached to its chest.

In front of the eight agile walking legs and behind the spider's tiny mouth is a pair of leglike structures called pedipalps. These work like fingers to grab and manipulate prey. The male spider also uses its pedipalps in the mating process.

In front of the pedipalps is a pair of chelicerae (ki-lis-e-ree), which end in sharp fangs. The fangs are the channels through which the spider injects digestive enzymes, as well as paralytic poisons, into its victims. Spiders lack chewing mouth parts and cannot eat solid food. Therefore, they dissolve the solid innards of a trapped insect and then suck out the liquefied nutrients.

A further comparison of insects and spiders reveals that insects have antennae and compound eyes. Spiders have neither of these. Tiny hairs that cover the spider's body are receptors that connect the spider with its world. Although they have from four to eight simple eyes, their vision is no match for the acute vision of insects. Many spiders don't need good eyesight because they work at night. Spiders that prowl in the daylight, such as jumping spiders, have better vision.

Perhaps the most characteristic feature of spiders is their webs and the silk they spin them with. Spiders have four to six silk glands located in their abdomens. Each gland produces a different kind of liquid silk. The spider uses

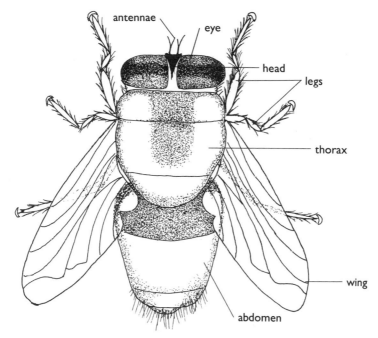

The greenbottle fly (family Calliphoridae) has a brilliant coppery green-colored body.

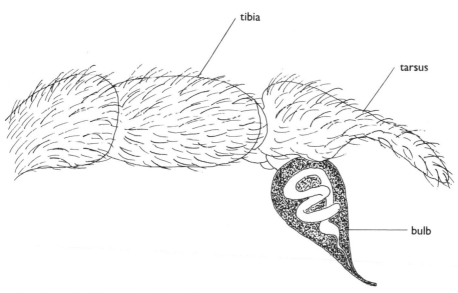

Pedipalps are leglike appendages that have become modified in the male to serve as copulatory organs. A reservoir in the male pedipalp is filled with sperm in preparation for mating.

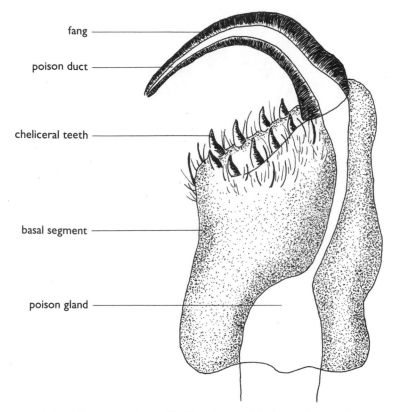

fang

poison duct

cheliceral teeth

basal segment

poison gland

Spiders use their chelicerae to bite and hold their prey. The bites of most spiders are not harmful to man.

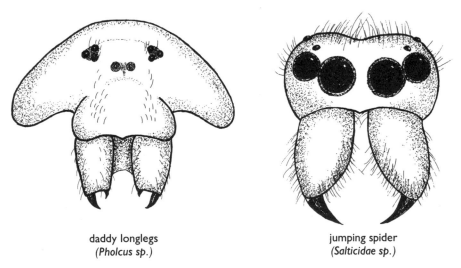

daddy longlegs
(Pholcus sp.)

jumping spider
(Salticidae sp.)

The facial arrangements of different species of spider vary greatly.

THE FOREST FLOOR

oonopid

tarantula

Spiders come in all sizes. Oonopids are less than 3mm (0.1") long, live under stones and can run very fast. Hairy mygalomorphs (tarantulas) may be as large as 9cm (3.5") with a 25cm (10") leg span. The largest spider in the United States may reach 7cm (2.7") and is found in Arizona. (Spiders are not drawn to scale.)

the various silks for its dragline and web construction. The silk is initially soluble in water, but as this complex liquid protein is stretched in the spinning process, it is converted into an insoluble material that can withstand a heavy dew or a spring shower.

Some of the silk threads are exceedingly strong. Arnachnologists believe the spider controls the strength of the threads by the way it draws them from its spinnerets. Spider thread is so thin that 250,000 of them laid side by side would span one inch. It is said to be as strong as an equal-sized strand of steel.

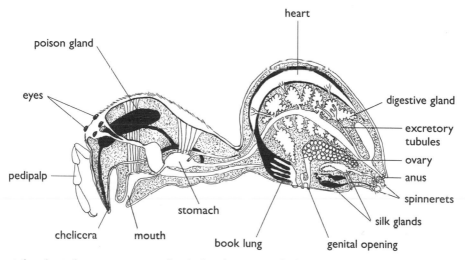

A female spider stores sperm in her body after mating for later fertilization of her eggs. The eggs are fertilized as they are deposited in one or more egg cases.

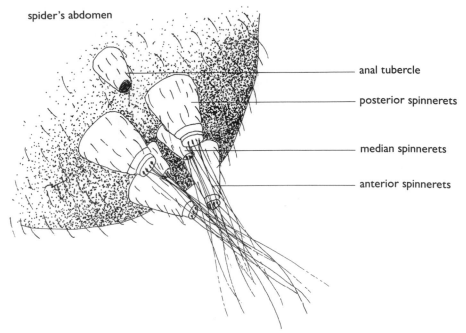

spider's abdomen

anal tubercle

posterior spinnerets

median spinnerets

anterior spinnerets

Spiders generally have three pairs of spinnerets.

Other threads are very sticky. Still others are so elastic that they can stretch up to twice their length and recoil undamaged.

Some spider species prefer to eat the old web and build anew rather than repair a tattered one. Researchers, with the help of radioactive tracers, have discovered that the protein in the ingested silk is recycled and becomes the building material for new webs, not new spider parts.

Many people associate spiders with webs, but spiders can do other remarkable things with their silk. One of the last projects of a spider's life is to spin an egg sac to hold the eggs that will produce the next generation of spiders. Often you can find these sacs in fields and meadows, attached to dead thistle stalks and other dried stems. You might also find some of these egg sacs in ceiling corners and other quiet nooks in your house.

Life in an egg sac is not snug and tranquil for the developing spiders. Inside each sac there is a life-and-death struggle going on. The stronger spiderlings devour the weak, and only they will survive the winter.

In the spring tiny spiderlings break through the wall of the sac that nurtured them through the winter and get ready to perform one of the most wondrous events in nature. The process, called ballooning, disperses the spiderlings to new habitats where they will mate, reproduce, and die. In preparation for the journey the tiny spiders scramble up blades of grass or the tips of twigs on small bushes. These places will serve as launch spots. Standing with their abdomens tilted toward the heavens, they begin to spin clusters of silken threads. The gentlest of breezes lifts the spiders from the earth and carries the tiny pioneers away. The young spiders usually float about two hundred feet above the ground and travel just a few miles from their birthplace.

A spider also uses silk for its dragline or securing line. The spider uses this line to transport itself from place to place by spinning out the appropriate kind of silk and securing it to something solid, such as a twig or stone. With a firm hold on this foundation, the spider feeds out a length of line and drifts on it to a new location. Probably you have seen a spider drop from a ceiling, dangle for a moment, then pull itself back to safety like a yo-yo on a string.

We all know that spiders use their silk to build webs or snares. The snares most often associated with spiders are the beautiful, circular webs of the orb weavers (family Araneidae). These engineering marvels are the most highly developed of all spider snares.

Are spiders dangerous? Spiders are very timid and most of them don't bite.

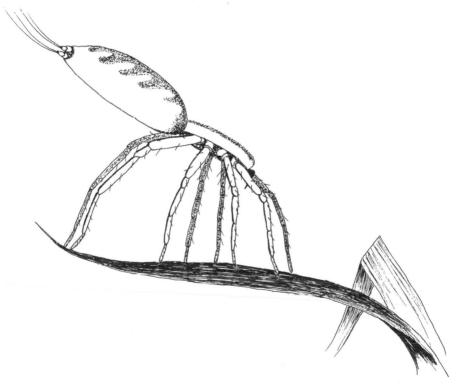

Spiderlings utilize the gentlest of breezes to balloon to a new home.

Of the three thousand species in North America, only the black widow spider and the brown recluse spider produce poisonous toxins. A bite from either of these spiders is painful, but it is more like a bee sting than a rattlesnake bite.

Spiders perform a wonderful service for us. They eat huge numbers of mosquitoes, flies, moths, and other insects and are nature's way of keeping populations of these pests in balance.

THE WORLD OF SPIDERS

What to Bring	Science Skills
basic kit	*observing*
flashlight	*measuring*
	recording
	comparing

OBSERVATIONS

Spiders can be found almost anywhere, but the easiest way to locate one is to find the web. The web will also give you clues to the identity of the spider that may be lurking nearby.

Webs and Their Weavers. The architecture of webs and the spiders that build them vary considerably. To help you organize what may seem a complex tangle of silk, put the webs you find into one of the following categories: cobweb, sheet web, funnel web, or orb web. The owners of these webs are often close by and, with patience and a bug box, you can usually get a good look at them.

Cobwebs. Certain spiderwebs are called cobwebs. These untidy tangles of threads usually hang from ceiling corners. Look in the attic, under the cellar stairs, or beneath water pipes and heat ducts that run across your basement ceiling. These webs were probably built by the house-loving comb-footed spiders (*Achaearanea tepidariorum*). The disheveled appearance of the webs belies the careful planning that went into their construction.

Use a flashlight to examine closely the structure. Is it the same thickness throughout? How is it held in place? Is there more than one layer?

You'll see a maze of silk and very often guy lines extending from corner posts and other supporting structures that hold the cobweb in place.

A region in the cobweb that's somewhat thicker than the rest of the web often serves as a shelter for the tenant. You will often find it hanging on the underside of the web. Its small tan body blends well with the dust-covered web. Gently blow on the web. What does the spider do?

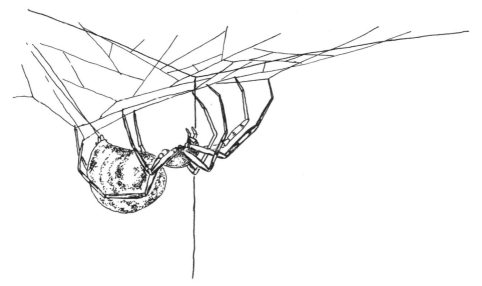

The American house spider is the architect and builder of the rough-looking silk traps that we call cobwebs.

Capture the spider in your bug box. Can you see the combs on its legs? These are used to toss the silk threads around its prey. (See Chapter Note 1, on comb-footed spiders.)

Are there small bundles hanging from the web by silk threads? These are probably egg sacs. How many are there?

After hatching from the egg sacs, the young spiders remain with their mother who feeds them regurgitated food. The spiderlings often stay with her until she dies and then devour her body immediately after her death.

Another cobweb spider you can find in your house is the long-bodied cellar spider (*Pholcus* sp.). Look for its cobwebs in the same kinds of places as the webs of comb-footed spiders. Often confused with daddy longlegs, or harvestmen, the long-bodied cellar spider has two body segments. The harvestman's body doesn't have any divisions.

You also can find cobwebs outside. Look for them on rock piles, on fences, and in shrubs.

Sheet Webs. Sheet webs are abundant in meadows and in shrubbery of fields and woods. This web is a closely woven horizontal platform a few inches from the ground and is about eight inches long. Observe the design of the platform. How many guy lines are there and to what are they attached?

Below the sheet or hiding in a retreat close by, a very small spider waits for an insect to get tangled in the mesh. Drop a live fly or beetle onto the gauze

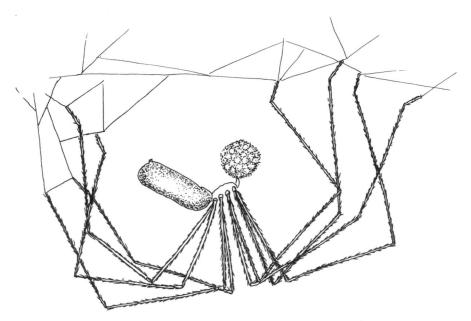

The female daddy longlegs (Pholcus sp.) holds the egg sac containing her young in her chelicerae.

platform. What happens? Follow the sequence and record it. (See Chapter Note 2, on sheet webs.)

Different species build different kinds of sheet webs. Look for these varieties called *bowl*, *doily web*, and *filmy dome*.

Funnel Webs. Another group of small spiders is the grass spider. Some of these grow to about three quarters of an inch. Grass spiders weave funnel webs. The top of the web is a flat sheet of silk and the bottom is shaped like a funnel, wide at one end and narrow at the other.

Look for these webs in grasses and low bushes early in the morning when the sun sparkles on the dew-drenched threads. To what are they attached? Where does the spider hide?

How strong is the platform? Trap several flies or beetles and then toss the insects one by one onto the platform. How many insects will the platform hold?

Orb Webs. Web construction reaches its zenith with the orb webs spun by garden spiders. Unlike other webs, the orb web is built vertically. This design works well for trapping flying insects. Although the basic design of the orb is similar to a wagon wheel, there are many variations on this basic plan.

Find an orb web. Which silk lines are the supporting beams, or frame-

Sheet webs are engineering marvels.

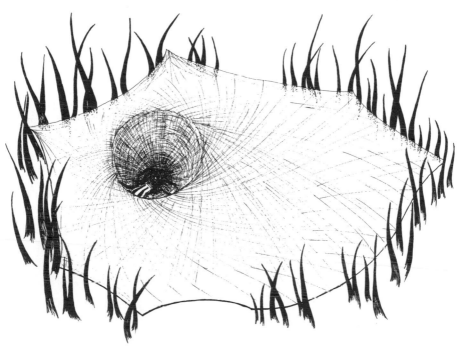

Spiders that construct funnel webs are found in grass and in low bushes.

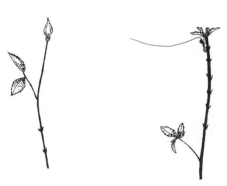 

To construct an orb web, the spider first lets out a length of silk and waits for the wind to carry it across the gap to form a bridge.

Next the spider lets out a loose thread and drops another from the center to form a Y. She attaches the end of this to a third support.

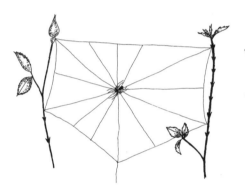 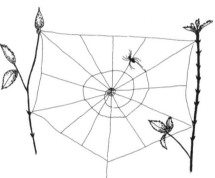

Next the spider makes a small platform in the center. From here the spider will be able to move quickly to any location on the web.

Working outward from the platform, the spider starts a temporary spiral of dry silk, which will be replaced by a permanent adhesive spiral.

work, of the web? Look for the guy lines that hold the framework to supporting objects. How many are there? To what are they attached?

Building a Web. How does the spider begin its web? Follow the building process from beginning to end. How many spirals are there? Are the spaces between the spirals equal? How many spokes are there? Describe the ribbon. How long did it take the spider to spin its web?

Look at several orb webs and compare them for the number of spokes, number of spirals, and the design of the ribbons.

If there isn't a spider in an orb web you find, tickle the web with a blade of

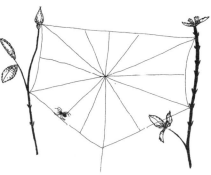

A radius thread, attached at the hub, is carried up to the bridge and then down a short distance before it is tightened and fastened.

Gradually she adds more threads to the hub until she completes the wheel-like frame. These silk radii help to stabilize the web.

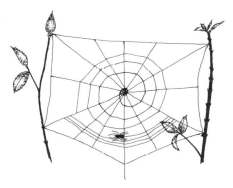

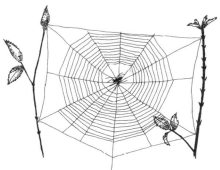

When the temporary spiral is complete, the spider reverses direction and spins the permanent spiral of closer-spaced, sticky strands.

When this second spiral has been completed, the spider sits behind the hub and waits for its prey.

grass. Does a spider suddenly appear? How did it know something was on its web?

Are the threads of the web sticky? Find out by gently touching the spokes and the spirals with some teased cotton. What did you learn? (See Chapter Note 3, on orb webs.)

It takes persistence and patience to find egg sacs. Look under loose pieces of tree bark, in a log pile, or in other protected spots for a sticky mass resembling cotton candy. It might be the cocoon made by a grass spider (*Agelenopsis*).

Scientists think ribbons woven in a spider's web may ward off low-flying birds. Different types of orb spiders create specific ribbon designs in their webs.

A tan ball, about one inch in diameter, attached by thin threads to weed stalks and other vegetation may be the egg sac of a garden spider (*Arigope* sp.).

Spiders That Don't Weave Webs. Hunting spiders, such as wolf spiders and jumping spiders, don't build silken snares or webs.

Wolf Spiders (*Lycosidae*). These bold hunters are among our most common spiders. Their name comes from *lycosa*, the Greek word for wolf. With its long legs and good eyesight, the wolf spider is built for a predatory lifestyle.

Look for them in the leaf litter, under stones, under pieces of bark, and among dead leaves. Their mottled brown bodies are well camouflaged, so they are most easily seen when running.

Compare the relative length of the wolf spider legs to that of a garden spider. Which has the longest legs?

Not all wolf spiders work during the day. A common species of wolf spider, the Carolina wolf spider (*Lycosa carolinensis*), hides by day and hunts by night. Another night hunter is the forest wolf spider (*Lycosa gulosa*).

As wolf spiders run along the ground, you might see them dragging a saclike object. This is an egg case. After hatching, the spiderlings ride piggy-back on the adult until they are able to hunt for themselves.

Crab Spiders. Crab spiders can move rapidly backward and sideways. This is one of the few features they share with crustaceans. Look for these crafty spiders on milkweed and goldenrod plants early in the summer. Since

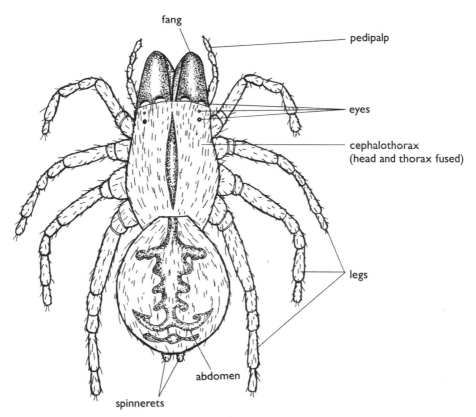

fang

pedipalp

eyes

cephalothorax
(head and thorax fused)

legs

abdomen

spinnerets

Jumping spiders have better vision than the nocturnal spiders.

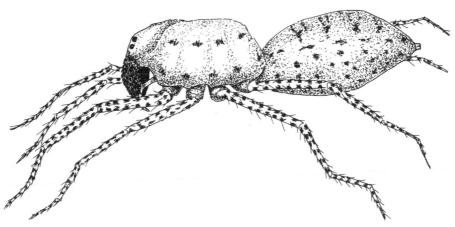

Its long legs help the wolf spider catch its prey.

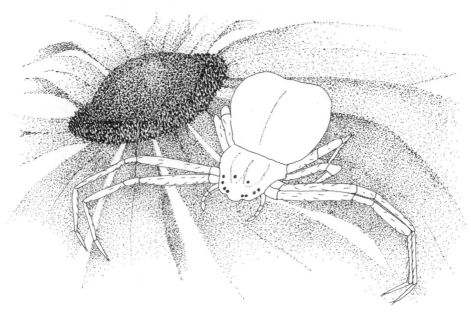

A crab spider waits in ambush for passing insects.

the color of the spider blends with the blossoms of the plants, it may take some time to find one.

Observe the crab spider move. How is its leg arrangement different from other spiders?

Trap-door Spiders. Spiders in this group make underground burrows, which they cover with a trapdoor. Long spines on the spider's chelicerae serve as rakes used to tunnel into the soil. The spider keeps its burrow opening covered with a hinged disk made of soil and grasses and some silk. When an insect strolls over the door, the vibrations alert the spider below. This agile

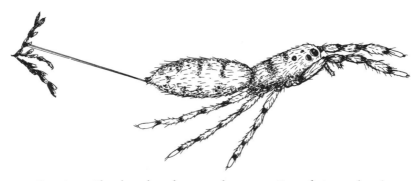

Jumping spiders have been known to leap many times their own length.

predator opens the trapdoor. Its front legs grab the prey and pull it inside, and the spider has a meal. Some trap-door spiders chase their prey. Trap-door spiders often line their earthen tubes with silk.

The trap-door spiders are regional spiders and are found primarily in the southeast.

Jumping Spiders. These colorful spiders are active during the day and can be identified by their irregular gait. They are agile, difficult to capture, and capable of leaping great distances relative to their size. Their family name, Salticidae, is from the Latin word for leap.

Draglines are paid out and attached to a firm substrate before each leap. Should the spider miss its intended victim, it can reel itself in and prepare for another leap. If you have a chance to observe a jumping spider, find out how far it can leap.

CHAPTER NOTES

1. Comb-footed Spiders. After the prey has been trapped by sticky threads, the comb-footed spider begins to spin, with the help of its combs, the heavy lines that will wrap the prey. Comb-footed spiders have been known to trap, wrap, and lift animals as large as small mice. This is possible because of the strength of the silk and the engineering skill of the tiny spider.

2. Sheet Webs. When the insect is thoroughly enmeshed, the spider pulls it through the webbing in the sheet. Often the spider will build a second platform below the first sheet to protect itself from attack below. The spider hides at the narrow end of the sheet. This opening also serves as a back door should the spider need to escape.

3. Orb Webs. The spokes, guy lines, and hub of the orb web are not sticky. Neither are they made from elastic threads. The sticky and elastic threads are used to make the spiral lines. When an insect becomes stuck to the spiral, it struggles to free itself only to find that it's making the problem worse. The spider is aware of the activity in the web through a taut trap line that transmits vibrations from the web to the retreat. The vibrations are received by the resident spider, who dashes to the scene. The spider either eats its prey on the spot or wraps the victim and stores it for a later meal.

Spiders don't stick to their own webs because their claws are protected by a thin film of oil. The oil, produced by special glands within the spider, is delivered by oil ducts to the claws as needed.

CHAPTER 13

Centipedes and Millipedes

HOW TO GET ALONG

Spring is a time of accelerated activity for plants and animals, as well as people. Look beneath decaying logs, leaf litter, and assorted rocks as you go about on your springtime forays. There you'll find a profusion of life forms emerging from their winter torpor. You might be startled by a profusion of spiders and insects scurrying to hiding places. In the wake of your intrusion you'll see some of these soil animals run for cover while others amble gracefully away.

Plant-eating millipedes and meat-eating centipedes are among the creatures you'll probably find. Superficially similar, these two very different members of the myriapod (many-legged) group are often confused with one another.

The ancestors of millipedes and centipedes were among the first animals to leave the relative stability of an aquatic life. They found a home roaming over the soil of the great, humid, coal-forming forests of the Carboniferous period, some two hundred fifty million years ago. Evolutionary biologists believe that this aquatic ancestor was a segmented worm that lived in ancient woodland pools. Those pools were alternately drenched by torrential rains and dried by the blazing sun. It was there, in dramatically changing environments, that myriapods evolved.

Like their arthropod cousins, both millipedes and centipedes sport firm exoskeletons, which protect the soft interior body parts beneath. This armor is periodically shed and replaced with a larger size as the animal grows. This is where the similarities end, however. The millipede's exoskeleton is stiff and contains a high percentage of calcium. Millipedes know instinctively that their diets must include high-calcium plant material. They are found in greater numbers where soils contain significant amounts of this element. The centipede's protective covering is made from a protein material called chitin. Low in calcium, chitin is very flexible. The centipede can extend, shorten, and flatten itself as the need arises. This is an advantage for a predator that must wiggle into tight crevices to find its next meal.

Millipedes and centipedes are not quite free of their watery past. Neither has managed to develop effective structural devices for controlling water loss. Unlike ants and some other arthropods, millipedes and centipedes don't have waxy coatings on their exoskeletons to help them retain moisture. Instead they have to protect themselves from water loss by a repertoire of behavioral strategies. For example, they live only in dark, humid places. Should these places dry out, the myriapods reflexively begin to search for damper digs. They seek shelter from the light by hiding under stones, pieces of bark, and leaf litter. The damp, litter-strewn forest floor or backyard garden suits them well.

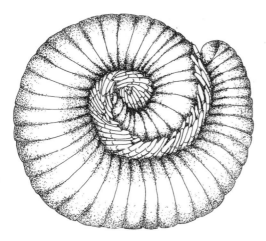

A coiled millipede protects its soft body parts with its hard outer covering.

Both millipedes and centipedes have jointed legs. The number, arrangement, and other characteristics of the legs of these two creatures is quite different. (See Chapter Note 1, on legs.) Centipedes have only one pair of legs on each of the leg-bearing segments. Their legs are exceptionally long and slender, just right for the high-speed chases that mark their predatory life-style.

In contrast, the millipede has two pairs of short, stubby legs on each body segment except for the first four. This twin-footed design is the result of the fusion of leg-bearing segments that occurs while the millipede develops inside the egg. This fusion makes it possible for the exoskeleton to stand up to the forces required for burrowing. Diplopoda, the name of the millipede group, reflects this double-footed design.

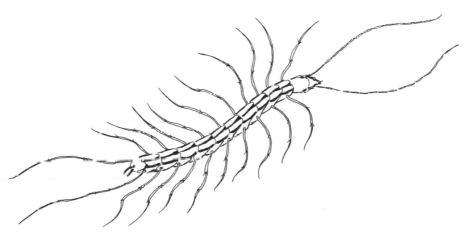

Centipedes, like this house centipede (Chilopod), have flexible exoskeletons that allow them to squeeze into tight spaces in search of food.

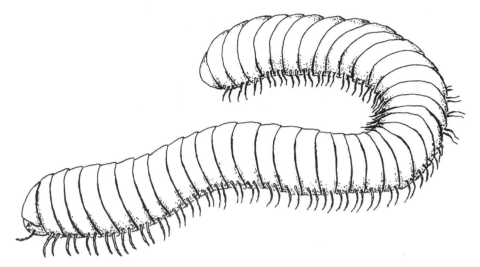

Millipedes (class Diplopoda) *have hard, calcium-rich exoskeletons to protect themselves from predators.*

The extra legs give millipedes power to push through the soil and leaf litter. They do not use their legs uniformly in the effort, however. The number of legs used in each pushing stroke depends on the force needed to move the animal through the litter. If the millipede encounters resistance, it puts more legs into operation. Despite their extra legs, millipedes are not nearly as quick as centipedes. Their movements are slow and quite graceful. Fortunately they don't need a rapid getaway to escape their predators. (See Chapter Note 2, on defenses.)

The differences between the legs of millipedes and those of centipedes betray the differences in food sources. Millipedes are slow-moving scavengers of the woodland floor. Their bodies are cylindrical, almost wormlike. The design of the millipede head makes it easy for the creature to slog through the soil surface. Its mouthparts can tear and chew litter with remarkable efficiency. Unable to break down the stiff cellulose of leaves on their own, millipedes prefer plant material that has already been partially digested by fungi and bacteria. Millipedes are important members of the woodland nutrient-recycling team. With the help of other soil creatures, such as pill bugs and sow bugs, millipedes are responsible for reducing about one-twentieth of the huge annual leaf fall.

Centipedes are members of a group called Chilopoda. The name refers to the centipede's lobsterlike claws. These first two claws are not used for running. They have been modified for grasping prey. The claws, so effective at holding and tearing such prey as silverfish and cockroaches, project forward. They are sharp and contain poison ducts, which secrete chemicals used to kill prey.

Millipedes and centipedes offer an exquisite example of how two related creatures can share the same habitat and still remain in harmony with one another. The answer to this tranquility lies in the behavioral and structural strategies that each uses for survival: They have no need to compete with each other for life's necessities.

THE WORLD OF CENTIPEDES AND MILLIPEDES

What to Bring
basic kit
baking pan
soil
watch with second hand
tweezers
drawing paper
shoe box

Science Skills
observing
comparing
inferring
recording

OBSERVATIONS

You will need to trap a few centipedes and millipedes for these observations, but don't collect them until you're ready to use them. Centipedes have been known to eat each other when no other food is available, so put each in its own container. Because they are plant eaters, millipedes can be put in the same container. Keep a piece of moist paper toweling in with your creatures.

Millipede or Centipede? People often confuse millipedes and centipedes. After observing them for a while you will be able to tell the difference.

Centipedes are very active and often won't keep still long enough for you to observe them closely. Exposure to cold slows them down, so put your centipedes (in their container) into the refrigerator. Leave them there for a few hours.

In the meantime capture a millipede, the bigger the better. To get a good look at its head, gently grasp it with pair of tweezers. How many antennae does it have? Are they long or short? Are they straight or curved? Does the millipede keep them close to its head, or does it wave them around? The antennae are equipped with tiny hairs designed to detect odors. Use a hand lens for a better look.

How many body segments does your millipede have? How many legs are

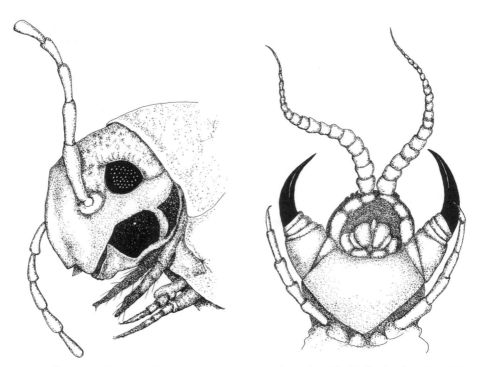

The millipede, with its simple eyes and antennae, tucks its head behind a hardened shield when burrowing. The first trunk segment of the centipede incorporates a pair of poisonous claws.

on each segment? What is their relative length? Describe the millipede's movements. How does it use its legs when it walks? Place a small mound of soil in its path. Does it use its legs differently when it meets your obstacle? How does this help the millipede to shove its way through the soil? Is its body round, oval, or flat?

Remove the centipede from the cold. Compare it with the millipede. What are the similarities and differences? Begin with the head, antennae, legs on each segment, length of legs, leg movements, and body shape. Watch a centipede move in the leaf litter or in a flat container. Compare it with the movement of a millipede.

Pay attention to the behavioral differences between the two species. Which would you say is the more aggressive?

EXPLORATIONS

Marvelous Millipedes. Put a millipede on a three-foot-square piece of drawing paper. As it begins to explore, trace its path with a magic marker.

Is its path straight, curved, or a squiggle? Put the millipede back at the starting point. Does it follow the same path this time?

Arrange the paper so that only half is in the sun. Does the millipede travel away from the sun or toward it? Try this a few more times. Can you find a pattern to the millipede's movements?

Put the millipede in a shoe box. Where does the millipede spend most of its time? In the middle of the box or crawling along the edge?

Collect a few millipedes. Put them, one at a time, on a large open space, such as the floor. What is the average distance your millipedes will crawl in one minute?

Try this exploration with centipedes. You will want to contain them inside barriers, so that they don't disappear.

Myriapods and Open Spaces. You have probably found your centipedes snuggled into some pretty tight spaces, such as under the bark of a rotting log or under a rock. Find out what the centipede does when no tight spaces are available.

Get a deep-sided container, such as a baking pan. Put about an inch of soil in it. Then put a centipede in the center of the container. What does the centipede do in the absence of snug hiding places? Where does it go? How long does it spend in each spot? Do other centipedes respond the same way?

Remove the centipede and add some leaf litter and several pieces of tree bark to the container. Put the centipede back into the center of the container. What does it do now? Do other centipedes respond in a similar way?

Try the same investigation with millipedes. Do they seek out snug spaces in the same way that centipedes do?

Myriapods and Moisture. Put some soil in the baking pan. Divide the pan in half with a waterproof barrier, such as a ruler, that is not higher than the soil surface. Moisten one half of the soil. Put a millipede on the dry side. What happens? How long does the millipede take to act?

Try the same exercise with a centipede. Does it react in the same way as the millipede? On which side of the pan do the myriapods spend most of their time?

If you want to observe both millipedes and centipedes at the same time, put them in separate pans. A hungry centipede that is unable to find other food may make a meal of the lumbering millipede.

CHAPTER NOTES

1. **Facts about Legs.** The number of legs a myriapod possesses is not very closely related to its name. The greatest number of legs ever recorded for a millipede is not 1,000, but 750. A European centipede boasts 254 legs, rather than the mere 100 that its name implies.

2. **Defenses.** Myriapods have a wide array of defenses. Most centipedes

have simple eyes and light-sensitive receptors scattered over their bodies. These adaptations allow them to avoid light and thus capture by sighted predators. One species of centipedes leaves a chemical trail that emits a seductive iridescent glow. This luminescent substance can also sting a predator, persuading it to go elsewhere.

When disturbed or alarmed, some species of millipedes simply roll up and play dead. The animal's head, its tiny feet, and its soft underside are protected by the hard exoskeleton. Another group of millipedes secretes a gluey substance onto the ground that snares unsuspecting predators in a sticky web of goo. Still another species uses chemical weapons. A line of minute ducts, almost one to every segment, runs the length of the millipede body. When in danger, the millipede fires a spray of hydrogen cyanide from the ducts. It has good aim and only fires from the section of the body that faces the attacker. (This chemical is harmless to most organisms and to other millipedes.)

CHAPTER 14

Fungi

A FUNCTIONAL BEAUTY

The stubborn molds and mildews that appear in the shower, around the kitchen, and in the basement, are fungi. Miracle drugs like penicillin are derived from fungi. That famous gourmet mushroom, the truffle, which sends small bands of devotees on annual treks into the forest, is a fungus. Although the mildews, molds, and mushrooms in our homes, gardens, and forests are very different from each other in shape, size, and texture, they all belong to the same huge biological kingdom.

Some people think mushrooms are downright ugly. For them, mushrooms are dull, drab objects that hide in the leaf litter or pop up mysteriously, spoiling carefully tended lawns. There are others, however, who feel that the yellows, reds, and oranges of mushrooms add a splash of color to the autumn forest litter. If you look beyond the obvious, you'll find that an exquisite functional beauty belies the exterior of even the most dingy in the clan.

The textbook mushroom, with its stalk, cap, and gills, is the only visible product of an underground life cycle drama that began several months, years, or even centuries earlier. On the underside of a mushroom cap are thin, radiating blades of tissue called gills. The gills house structures that produce millions of lightweight, microscopic spores. People often compare spores to seeds, although spores are structurally less complex and do not contain food or plant embryos as seeds do. Spores do function like seeds to produce new generations of fungi. Because mushrooms produce the spores, they are the reproductive phase of a very intricate life cycle.

When spores reach maturity, millions of them are released. Some dispersed spores settle close to the parent mushroom, but most are carried by air currents to distant places. Those spores that find conditions with adequate moisture and sufficient nutrients will germinate.

Each developing spore produces a mycelium. The mycelium is a mass of tangled, white, tubular threads. The single threads are called hyphae. As each hypha branches and rebranches again and again, the visible mycelium is formed. Sometimes you can find this soft mycelial mat if you peel away pieces of bark from a rotting log or if you turn over the soil close to some sprouted mushrooms.

The mycelium is the main body of the fungus we call a mushroom. The threads of the mycelium meander through the soil, absorbing food and building nutrient reserves. Mycologists (students of mushrooms) don't know exactly how long a mycelium must grow before mushroom formation can begin, but when the control mechanisms are finally triggered, some tiny cells in the mycelium begin to specialize. Mycelium knots or tangles about the size of a

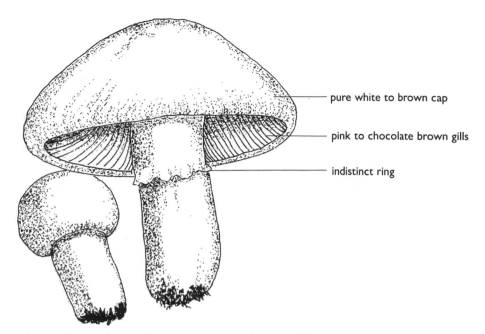

- pure white to brown cap
- pink to chocolate brown gills
- indistinct ring

The meadow mushroom (Agaricus campestris) is an edible variety that is widely cultivated.

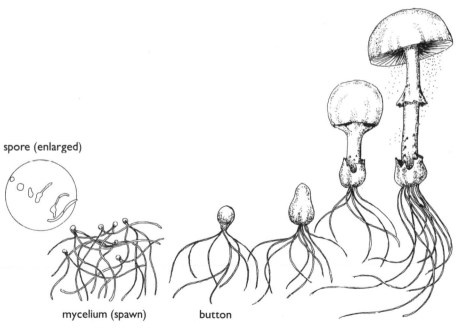

spore (enlarged)

mycelium (spawn)   button

Gilled mushroom formation begins when cells in the mycelium specialize, creating knots or tangles that eventually develop into the familiar caps and stalks of mature fungi.

pinhead develop. The threads that make up these tangles are specialized so that, even at this stage, the destiny of each has been determined. Some will become the stalk, some the cap, some the gills, and some the spores. The knot gradually becomes club-shaped and may be surrounded by a protective membrane as it grows toward the soil surface. The stalk grows longer and the upper end of the knot swells as the structure gradually assumes the shape of the familiar mushroom cap and stalk.

Although the mushroom "button" remains small, it continues to develop just under the soil. At this point all of the mushroom parts are present, but they are not yet full-size. The button is either at ground level or barely above the soil surface, and the mushroom goes unnoticed. Following a long, gentle rain or a sudden deluge, the buttons absorb the available water and swell to their full height. A full stand of mushrooms appears, as if by magic, where none was seen before.

The familiar mushroom is the result of a long period of underground mycelial activity. Without the nutrient-absorbing threads, the mushroom would not exist and the fungus could not produce offspring.

Unlike green plants, fungi are unable to capture solar energy for use in the manufacture of organic compounds like fats and sugars. Instead, the growing tips of the mycelial threads secrete digestive enzymes into the soil. These chemicals come in contact with minerals and energy-rich organic matter and dissolve them. The dissolved matter is then absorbed into the body of the fungus similar to the way roots of green plants take in water. This ability to break down plant and animal material for food makes fungi part of the earth's cleanup crew.

THE WORLD OF FUNGI

What to Bring	Science Skills
basic kit	*observing*
pen knife	*recording*
	grouping
	comparing

OBSERVATIONS

Look for fungi on decaying tree branches in fields, vacant lots, along the roadside, and in your backyard. Although you will see some kinds of fungi on living vegetation, you can expect to find more fungi wherever there is dead organic material. Old fallen logs are a favorite mushroom habitat.

Take a notebook on your fungi hunt so that you can record a brief description of them and when and where you found them. A camera with a close-up lens will help you keep an accurate record.

You can find fungi throughout the year. Woody pore or bracket fungi, such as artists fungi (*Ganoderma applanatum*), project from tree trunks like small shelves. They remain there for years and are easily located. In the spring you might find the prunelike caps of the morels (*Morchella esculenta*). These gourmet mushrooms are usually a little more difficult to find, because their yellowish-tan caps are well camouflaged in the leaf litter on the forest floor. Autumn is the most popular season for fungi hunting. To find a bumper crop, do your fall hunting after it rains.

Fungi are grouped according to the location of their spore factories. Using this criterion, mycologists have identified four major groups in the fungi system: basidiomycetes, gastromycetes, ascomycetes, and heterobasidiomycetes. Each of these groups probably contains some familiar fungi, but it is helpful to learn some of the distinguishing characteristics.

Basidiomycetes. In this group, spores are produced within structures on the underside of the mushroom cap. This surface may display a collection of tiny holes or it may consist of thin sheets of tissue called gills radiating from the center. There are six different categories of fungi in this group: gilled, pored, chanterelle, coral, teeth, and polypore. You will find many exceptions to the descriptions that follow. They are merely guidelines for you to use as you begin your adventures in the world of fungi.

Gilled Mushrooms. There are a very large number of species of gilled mushrooms. Color, shape, texture, size, odor, structural characteristics, and other details are used to identify these mushrooms.

Observe the color of the cap. Is it red, like the fly agaric (*Amanita muscaria*) or the pungent russula (*Russula emetica*)? Is it lilac or purple, like the clean mycena (*Mycena pura*)? Is it brownish orange, like the lactarius orange (*Lactarius volemus*)?

What is the shape of the cap? Are the caps of your fungi trumpet-shaped like chanterelles, or are they cone-shaped like the inky caps (*Coprinus* spp.) or the parasol mushrooms (*Lepiotas* spp.)? Is the center of the cap depressed, like the orange-brown lactarius (*Lactarius volemus*)? Is it convex, like the flat-topped meadow mushroom (*Agaricus placomyces*)?

The mushroom found most often on supermarket shelves (*Agaricus campestris*) is also a meadow mushroom with a rounded cap.

Look under the cap of the mushroom. What color are the gills? Are the gills the same color as the cap?

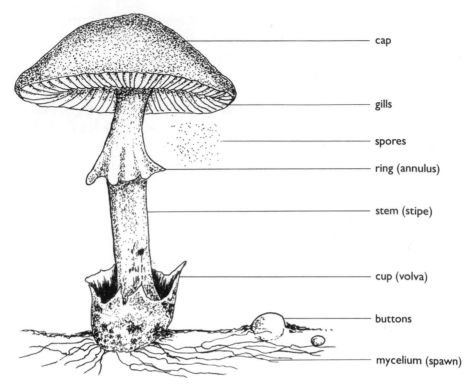

cap

gills

spores

ring (annulus)

stem (stipe)

cup (volva)

buttons

mycelium (spawn)

The radiating structures in which a mushroom's spores develop are clearly visible on this gilled mushroom.

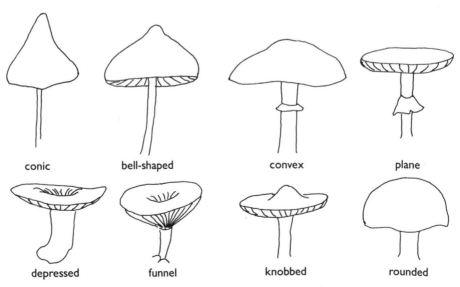

conic

bell-shaped

convex

plane

depressed

funnel

knobbed

rounded

The shape of a mushroom's cap can help to identify it.

When handled or injured, some mushrooms change color. The bleeding mycena (*Mycena haematopus*) oozes a red liquid when cut. This is a well-known gilled mushroom that thrives on the dead, decaying wood of deciduous trees. If you put a few drops of water mixed with caustic soda on the California field mushroom (*Agaricus californicus*), it turns yellow.

Observe the texture of a gilled mushroom. You'll find that some fungi are covered with a gelatinous slime, but that others have a velvety feel to them. Other mushrooms wear a thin film of powder. The caps of others are dotted with warts. Does the cap have scales?

Is the cap dry and hairy, like the dry tricholoma (*Tricholomopsis rutilans*)? Is the cap slimy when wet, like the honey mushroom (*Armillariella mellea*)?

How large is your fungus? A mushroom can be as tall as ten inches, like the green gill mushroom (*Chlorophylum molybdites*), or as short as two inches, like the short-stemmed russula (*Russula brevipes*).

Cut a gilled mushroom lengthwise to see the relationship between the gills and the stem.

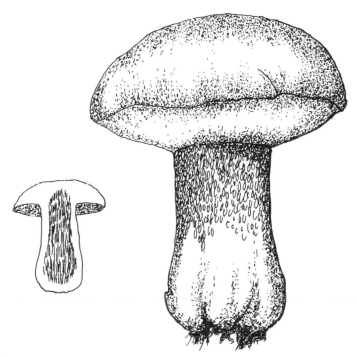

Flesh of the red-pored, blue-staining bolete (Boletus pulcherrimus) *turns blue when cut or bruised.*

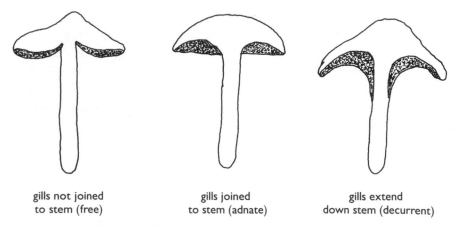

| gills not joined to stem (free) | gills joined to stem (adnate) | gills extend down stem (decurrent) |

The gills of a mushroom may or may not be attached to the stem.

Mushrooms in which the gills are not attached to stem are the aminitas, the smooth lepiotas (*Leucogaricus naucina*), and the horse mushroom (*Agaricus arvensis*).

If the gills are attached or partially attached, you probably have a rooting collybia (*Oudemanisella radicata*) or a clean mycena (*Mycena pura*).

Cottony-margined milky cap (*Lactarius deceptivus*) and delicious lactarius (*Lactarius deliciosus*) have gills attached and running down stem.

Notched gills indicate clustered inocybe (*Inocybe fastigiata*) or scaly pholiota (*Pholiota squarrosoides*). The gills of both of these species may be attached.

Spore color is another important clue for mushroom identification. Although it is impossible to see the color of a single spore without the aid of a microscope, a large number of them in one spot will reveal the color. Many field guides provide instruction for collecting spores.

Stems are also good aids in identification. Does your fungi have a stem, or is it attached directly to a log or tree? Does the stem swell near the base, like amanitas? Or is it of equal circumference throughout its length, like the meadow mushroom (*Agaricus campestris*)? Does the base of the stem seem to be sitting in a cup?

Cut the mushroom through its length. What does the inside of the stem look like? Is the stem hollow? Is it filled with a porous material? What is the texture of the stem? Is it hairy, scaly, smooth, or some other texture?

How do your mushrooms smell? If they have a fragrant odor, they might be maroon tricholomas (*Tricholomopis rutilans*). If the odor is foul, it could be the flat-topped meadow mushroom (*Agaricus placomyces*).

Tubed Mushrooms. Mushrooms in this group lack gills. On the underside of their caps you'll find a collection of holes or pores. The pores are the openings to a system of tubes in which the spores are produced. When mature, the spores are forcibly expelled from the pores.

The tubed mushrooms form a very colorful, varied group of fungi. Keep a record of the different places you find each kind of tubed mushroom. Is it found growing under all conifers or does it seem to grow only under specific conifers, such as pines, larches, or spruce? Does it grow under broad-leaved trees? If you find it growing on logs and tree stumps, what kind of trees were they?

Observe the color of the cap. Is it gray to black like that of old-man-of-the-woods *(Strobilomyces floccopus)?* Or is it brown like that of *Suillus luteus?*

What is the shape of the cap? Is it helmet-shaped like that of *Boletus*

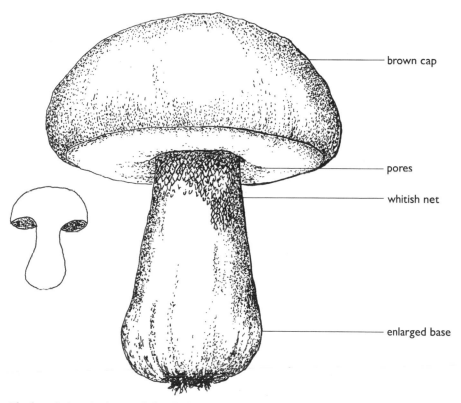

brown cap

pores

whitish net

enlarged base

The king bolete (Boletus edulis) *lacks gills but has spongy, whitish-yellow pores with very small openings for spore dispersal.*

luridus? Or is the cap somewhat pointed or knobbed like that of the American yellow bolete *(Suillus americanus)?*

Look under the cap of the mushroom. What color are the pores? Is the color the same as the top of the cap? Or is it different from that of painted bolete *(Suillus pictus)?*

With the help of your magnifier observe the pores. The shape and size of the pores will vary with the species of mushroom. Are the pores on your mushroom large or small? Are they round or angular?

Observe the texture of a tube mushroom. Does the cap feel sticky and slimy like that of Greville's bolete *(Suillus grevillei)?* Or is it hairy like that of the admirable bolete *(Boletus mirabilis)?* How many different textures can you find among the tubed mushrooms? How does that compare with what you found among the gilled mushrooms?

Some of the pored mushrooms change color when damaged. The painted bolete *(Suillus pictus)* will turn from yellow to brown, and the dull yellow underside of the American yellow bolete *(Suillus americanus)* will also turn brown when cut or bruised.

Observe the stem of your mushroom. Is it wider at the base than at the top like that of the king bolete *(Boletus edulis)?* Does it expand in the center like that of the orange bolete *(Liccinum aurantiacum)?* Is it hairy like the stem of *Boletus piperatus?* Is the circumference of the stem uniform?

Is the stem one color? Is the color at the base or at the top of the stem different from the rest of the stem? Are blotches present? Is there a netlike pattern on the stem like that of the bitter bolete *(Tylopilus felleus)?* Is the stem covered with colored dots like the reddish-brown dots on the whitish stalk of *Suillus granulatus?*

Polypore Fungi. Polypore fungi also have pores on their undersides. One observable difference between the two groups is their texture. Polypores are the woody or leathery shelflike growths you've seen growing out of tree trunks. They are often called bracket or shelf fungi.

How does the fungus feel? Is it hard, spongy, brittle, or leatherlike? Do you see a stem where the fungus joins the tree? Is the fungus growing alone or in a cluster?

What color is the fungus? Is it the same color on the upper surface as it is on the lower surface? Is the color on the surface uniform? If not, how would you describe the coloration?

How big is it? Is it the same thickness close to the tree trunk as it is at the outer edge?

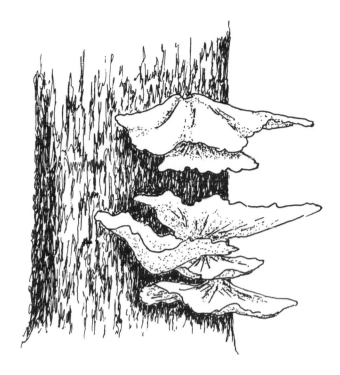

The sulfur-yellow shelf mushroom (Sulphur polyporus) grows in overlapping clusters on stumps, logs, or standing oaks.

Examine the undersurface with a magnifier. What do you see?

Find different kinds of bracket fungi and compare them to each other. What similarities and differences do you find?

Chanterelles. Many species of these delicious mushrooms can be identified by the fluted edges of their caps and their funnel shape. The gills of the chanterelles are more widely spaced than those of other gilled mushrooms. These blunt edged gills extend down the stem and are generally easy to see.

The color of the cap among chanterelles ranges from the dark brown of the deceptive chanterelle (*Craterellus fallax*) to the pale yellow of the smooth chanterelle (*Cantharellus lateritius*). You might even find the red-orange of the shaggy chanterelle (*Gomphus flocosus*) or the pale violet of pig's-ears (*Gomphus clavatus*).

The cap may have small brownish scales, as in the *Cantharellus tubae-formis*, or the scales may be orange, as in the shaggy chanterelle.

When you find one of these epicurean delights, record its location. Chanterelles tend to grow in the same place each year.

Teeth Fungi. These fungi may look like just another gilled mushroom, but a close look at the undersurface of the cap will tell you another story. Instead of gills you will see their distinctive teethlike spines, which produce the spores. Some of these fungi look like bracket or shelf fungi, but by their teeth you will know them.

Coral Fungi. You'll recognize some members of this group by their fingerlike stalks. Others resemble the coral animals you see in tropical waters. Some coral fungi look like brains. Others resemble small clubs.

Gastromycetes. The spores in this group of mushrooms are produced inside the fruiting body. There are four major groups of gastromycetes: stinkhorns, bird's-nest fungi, true puffballs, and earthstars.

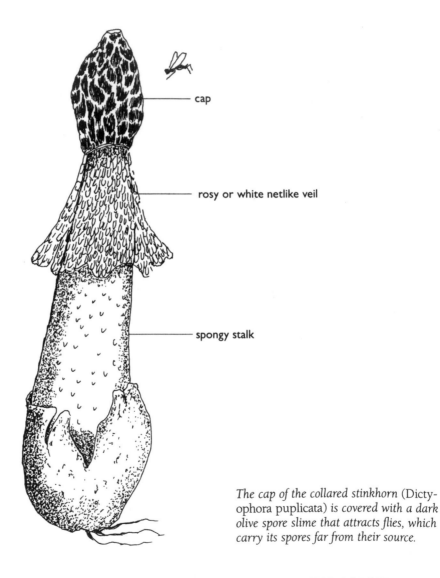

cap

rosy or white netlike veil

spongy stalk

The cap of the collared stinkhorn (Dictyophora puplicata) is covered with a dark olive spore slime that attracts flies, which carry its spores far from their source.

Stinkhorns. The hornlike stalk of stinkhorns begins developing inside an "egg" produced on strands of mycelium. At "hatching" time, the stinkhorn stalk breaks through the egg and in a few hours grows to its full length. For some species of stinkhorn, the stalk may grow its full height in as little as thirty minutes. The length of the stalk depends on the species; some grow to a height of six inches. The base of the egg becomes a cup, which the stalk sits in.

As for the odor of these fungi, their name says it all. Sometimes the smell of rotting meat signals the presence of stinkhorns. The spores of these fungi are produced inside the caps. When mature, the spores float to the surface on a foul-smelling liquid attractive to flies and other insects. The spores stick to the insects' feet, and as the insects dart from place to place, they spread the spores far from the stinkhorn.

If you can get close enough to stinkhorns, note the color and texture of the stalk.

What color is the tip? Does there appear to be any goo on it?

Bird's-nest fungi. These fungi resemble bird's nests replete with tiny "eggs." These eggs contain spores that are catapulted out of the nest by the force of falling raindrops. The nests usually grow in clusters, and each is about the size of a dime.

True Puffballs. These curious fungi sometimes appear as round, stemless objects. Other puffballs are pear-shaped and have thick, short stems. Both occur in grassy park areas and in woodlands. Children delight in stomping on puffballs because of the *pop* and the cloud of dust (spores) that shoots from them. You can find small puffballs growing out of rotting wood.

True puffballs range in color from white to yellow to orange. Some even have a smoky hue to them. What colors have you found?

Examine the surface of a puffball with a magnifier. Is it spiny? Are there any hairlike projections? Does it appear marbled?

Earthstars. When they first appear, earthstars resemble puffballs, but the outer skin of the earthstar ball peels back to form rays. The spores develop in the inner sphere. Look for earthstars on the soil surface and in the litter beneath broad-leaved trees.

Ascomycetes. The true morels are members of this group. These prune-headed fungi are exceptionally tasty. The spores are produced in structures on the upper surface of the ridged and pitted head.

False morels are also in this group, but they are poisonous. False morels can generally be identified by their furrowed, fissured, and irregularly-shaped caps. One species of false morel has a smooth, brown, saddle-shaped cap. The flesh of false morels is usually crisp and cracks easily.

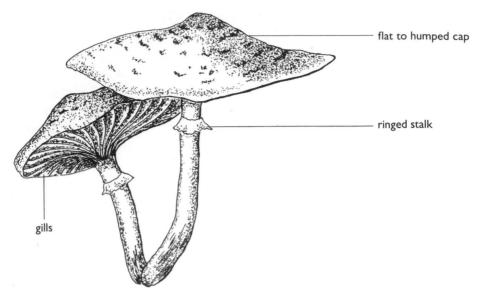

flat to humped cap

ringed stalk

gills

The mycelium of the honey mushroom (Armillariella mellea) *are bioluminescent. Its adnate gills release white spores from beneath scaly honey-yellow to reddish brown caps.*

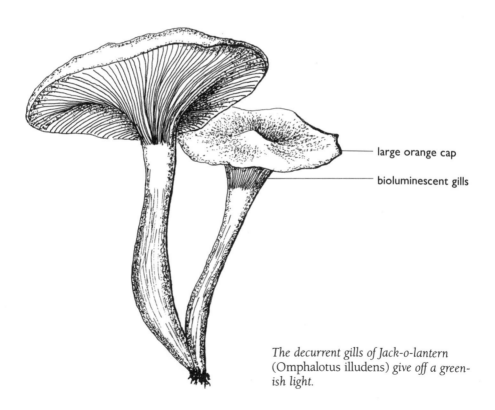

large orange cap

bioluminescent gills

The decurrent gills of Jack-o-lantern (Omphalotus illudens) *give off a green-ish light.*

Another type of ascomycete is the cup fungi. These look like tiny cups without handles. They are colorful and range in size from one eighth inch to four inches wide. Look for the yellow, blue-green, pink, scarlet, and orange cups on dead branches and even on packed soil along the roadsides.

Heterobasidiomycetes. Very often the fungi listed in this group are placed with the basidiomycetes. These include the jelly fungi, which look like blobs of jelly or butter when wet, though they are stiff and brittle when dry. Look for them on rotting logs, branches, and dead tree trunks. They can be yellow, white, black, or orange.

Foxfire and Other Woodland Ghosts. Mushrooms that glow in the dark? Mushrooms that cast an eerie light? Strange but true.

The best time for you to look for bioluminescence is at night. Explore around rotting tree stumps in the forest. You may have to kick at the decaying wood to see the luminescence.

Groups of the honey mushroom (*Armillaria mellea*), which grow on conifers and hardwoods, glow in the dark. Look for them at the base of the tree or on a rotting log. Since it is the mycelium of the mushroom that glows, you will have to peel away some of the bark to see it.

Another mushroom that has bioluminescent properties is the jack-o'-lantern (*Clitocybe illudens*). Take clusters of these mushrooms into a dark room. You'll see a soft, greenish light coming from their gills.

King bolete (*Boletus edulis*) and sulfur shelf mushroom (*Polyporus sulphureus*) have luminescent properties, as do some members of the genus *Mycena*.

Growing Your Own Mushrooms. If you would like to grow your own mushrooms, you can purchase a kit from Delta Education, Inc., P.O. Box 950, Hudson, NH 03051.

CHAPTER 15

Ants

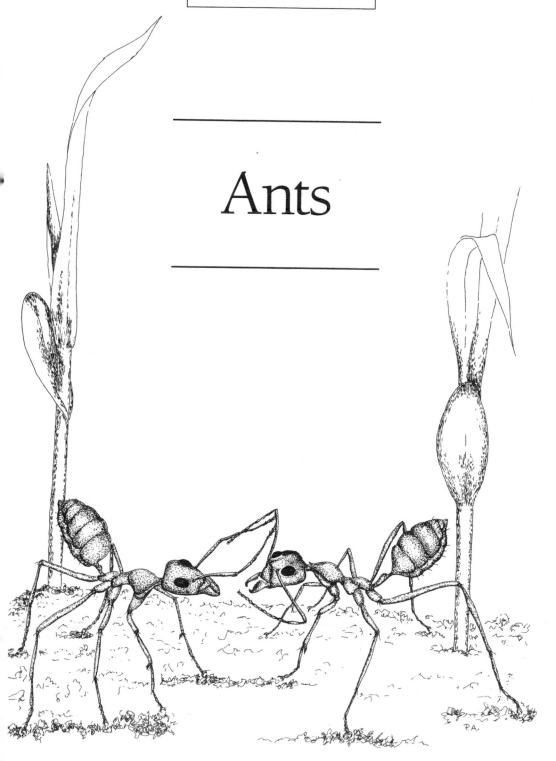

SURVIVAL IS NO PICNIC

Researchers estimate there are about 20,000 species of ants worldwide, and in each species there are billions of individuals. This biological success is largely due to the evolution of specialized behaviors and chemical mechanisms. Ants can flourish throughout an enormous range of temperatures, altitudes, moisture levels, and habitats, both natural and man-made. They thrive in nearly every available terrestrial nook except those permanently covered by snow.

Ants come in a variety of colors: black, brown, red, yellow, green, and combinations of these. They also display a dramatic range in size. One species of parasitic ant, which lives within the walls of nests made by larger ants, is only $1/25$ inch long, whereas the trocandria ants of South America measure a gigantic two inches in length. Our more familiar carpenter and field ants measure somewhere in between.

Ants are arthropods. Like all other arthropods ants have an external skeleton, jointed legs, and a divided body. But ants are a special kind of arthropod. As members of the insect class, they have three pairs of legs, paired wings, and three body divisions: head, chest, and abdomen.

Their exoskeleton is made of chitin. The young ant's outer layer of skin secretes this proteinaceous material. Once the protein hardens into jointed armor plates, the ant no longer grows. This external skeleton is equipped with a waxy coating, which helps prevent water loss. This process of skeletal formation differs from that of the crustacean arthropods, such as lobsters. A lobster sheds its external skeleton, climbs out, and produces a roomier one. The new exoskeleton is somewhat larger than the lobster's body size, thus allowing room for growth.

The fossil record indicates that ants were abundant during the Tertiary period some fifty million years ago. These earliest known ants had a caste system of queen, winged males, and immature female workers, the same highly advanced social behavior of ant colonies today. Each ant serves a function essential to the colony. It exists only for the benefit of the colony, and if removed from the group, it dies.

Scientists believe that ants evolved from a solitary, wasplike, flying insect that eventually developed social habits. Although bees and wasps remained capable of flight, ants went underground. Today most ant species nest beneath the soil, although some inhabit tree cavities and other natural hollows.

In response to declining temperatures, ground-nesting ants go deep into the soil and slowly drift into varying degrees of dormancy. They spend winter's most rigorous months in this state. Three to nine feet below the ground in galleries they've excavated, the ants are protected from freezing. In regions where snow remains deep throughout the winter, the snow insulates their somewhat shallower galleries.

Different species of ants differ in the constancy of their winter sleep. Those that dwell deep underground revive sooner than those ants, such as tree-dwellers, that are exposed to extreme temperatures.

Temperature influences much more than dormancy, however. In March, triggered by hormonal changes, ants wake from their winter torpor. The queen of the colony resumes egg laying. The workers busy themselves with the chores of the colony. Some of them care for the queen. Others tend to the eggs, keeping them clean and moving them from chamber to chamber to expose them to optimum incubation temperatures until they hatch. Workers also feed the ant larva. As the temperature continues to warm, these immature ants begin to pupate and finally develop into adult ants. Decisions about when to move the eggs from place to place, when to feed the larva, and when to leave the nest and forage for food are entirely chemically controlled.

THE WORLD OF ANTS

What to Bring
basic kit

Science Skills
observing
recording
inferring

OBSERVATIONS

The familiar ant is found throughout the world, so you can be sure there is a colony near you, whether you live in the city, the suburbs, or the woods.

A Close Look at Ants. The best way to find an ant is to sit down in the grass or on a decaying tree stump; the ants will soon find you. The large black, brown, or sometimes light reddish carpenter ants are easiest to examine. These ants usually live in the wood of dead trees or the wood of old houses. Capture one and put it into your bug box. Don't worry about taking your captive away from the colony. You will put it back where you found it when you're finished.

One of the first things you need to find out is whether you have trapped an ant or an ant look-alike.

Is your creature's body divided into three segments? Can you see its head, chest (thorax), and abdomen as three distinct divisions? If so, then it is an insect and may be an ant.

If you can see a waist between the chest and abdomen, then it is probably an ant and not a termite.

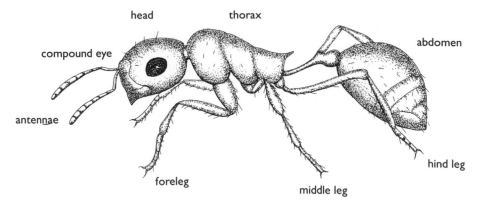

head   thorax

compound eye

antennae

foreleg

middle leg

abdomen

hind leg

The external structure of a typical ant (Formicidae) *clearly shows the waist between the thorax and the abdomen.*

Look at its antennae. Are they straight or do they have an elbow? If they have an elbow, your insect is an ant.

Ants or Termites? Although ants come from a line of wasps, they are often confused with termites, whose ancestors were more closely related to our present-day cockroaches. There are more than forty kinds of termites throughout our country. Unlike ants, which undergo complete metamorphosis through the four stages of egg, larva, pupa, and adult, termites develop in three stages: egg, nymph, and adult.

Termites lack a waist and are equipped with straight antennae. These two very different insects are confused most easily when they swarm. At that time the males of both groups fly, and their flight patterns are similar. Termites,

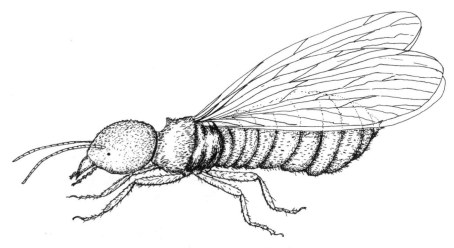

This winged termite is only one of more than forty species of termite.

queen ants, and male ants all have wings, but termites have two pairs of wings of equal length, and ants possess two pairs of wings of unequal length. If you can examine a winged termite, you will see why termites are often called white ants.

After the mating flight, winged male ants lose their wings and die. The queens either pull their wings off or abrade them on a rough surface. The muscle protein that controlled her wings is metabolized and used for egg production.

Ant Nests and Some Ant Behaviors. While observing the nests, you will have many opportunities to see some ant behaviors. You will probably add questions of your own to those below. Don't forget to take notes.

What do ants do with their antennae? (See Chapter Note 1, on antennae.)

Do ants appear to groom themselves? Observe the process. How long does it take? Why do you think grooming is important for the well-being of the ant colony?

When two ants meet, how do they interact? Does the interaction seem hostile? Friendly?

During what time of the day are the ants most active? Do they come out of the nest at night?

Put a large ant into a container. Using a 30 × illuminated magnifier, look closely at the ant's head. Look at the compound eyes and the large jawlike appendages. For what reasons do you think ants have these large jawlike structures? How do they use them?

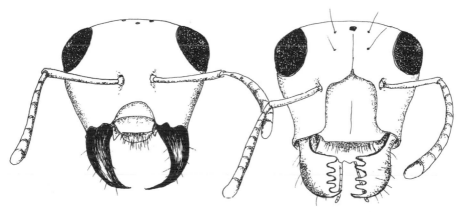

*Red Amazon ants have saber-shaped mandibles that are useful for fighting during slave raids, but useless for other kinds of work. Common black ants (*Formica sanguinea*) have unmodified mandibles with a full set of teeth on the gripping edge, enabling them to perform more varied tasks.*

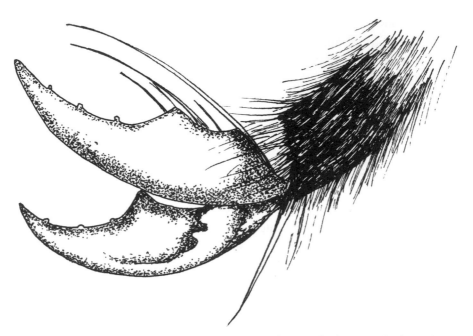

Most ants have hooked claws on their feet, allowing them to climb up tree bark or along the undersides of leaves.

Ants seem to defy gravity as they walk up walls and the legs of picnic tables. Look closely at their tiny "toes." How are they adapted for climbing? Do you think the toes help in grooming?

Are any ants carrying something? With the aid of your magnifier can you tell what it is? How do they manage to carry things and walk at the same time?

EXPLORATIONS

First One, Then Many. Make little piles of small fragments of food, such as meat, cake, sugar, or seeds. How long does it take one ant to find your food supply? What happens next? How many return together to the food source? How long did it take from the time you noticed the first ant until other ants were there? What kind of food did the ants carry away first?

Go to the Ant Mound. To discover something about the way ants live, you need to find a nest. How many openings are there in the nest? If there is more than one opening, how far apart are they? What campass direction do the openings face? How are these openings used by the ants?

How is the mound made? Is there loosely packed sand or soil? Is the top thatchlike, made of tiny twigs and grass? How tall is it? What is its diameter? What is the distance around the base of the nest?

How many holes are there in the nest? How do the ants use the different holes? How close is this nest to others? Are nearby nests occupied by the same kind of ant?

Look for other ant mounds. Where do you find them? In fields? Next to buildings? In the woods? In a park? Are they found more often in shady or sunny locations?

Find a mound and mark the place with some sort of flag. Make some notes about the characteristics of the mound.

Return to the nest in a day or two. Are there any changes in the shape or size of the nest? Are there other changes? Is there a change in the level of activity from one day to another? Has the temperature changed considerably since your last visit? How does a rain shower change the shape of the nest?

Who's Who on a Rotting Log? Find a decaying tree stump or tree limb lying on the woodland floor. Look for the large, black carpenter ants nearby. Pull off a piece of loose bark and you will probably find a colony of carpenter ants living in a maze of galleries, halls, and rooms.

Look for worker ants. These are the immature, wingless females. They feed and clean the queen. Can you find her?

Other female ants are nurses. They care for the larvae and pupae. Can you

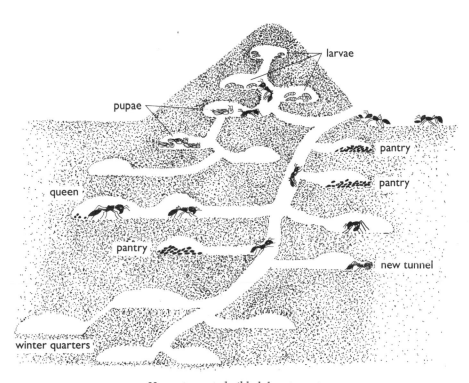

Harvester ants build elaborate nests.

find ant larvae and pupae? The pupae of some species are naked and helpless. When viewed with a magnifier, their tiny parts are visible. The pupae of other kinds of ants are wrapped in cocoons and are often mistaken for grains of rice.

Ants and Their Relationships. Locate some milkweed plants. Look under several leaves for colonies of aphids and a collection of ants. What do you observe to be the interactions between ants and aphids? (See Chapter Note 2, on the ant-aphid relationship.)

Some distance away from the first, look for another milkweed plant with aphids and ants in attendance. Are these ants from the same colony as those on the first plant you observed? To find out, remove an ant from one plant and place it near the ants on the other. What happens? Is the ant ignored by the others? Is it met with hostility?

Find out how many different ant colonies are feeding in a field of milkweed.

Look for the nest of one of these colonies. How far is it from the milkweed plants used by that colony?

If you cannot find any milkweed in your area, you can discover the same kind of ant-aphid relationship on viburnum. Viburnum can be found in woodlands and along rivers and creeks. A field guide will help you identify the shrub.

Ant Trails. You have observed that when one ant finds a food source, other

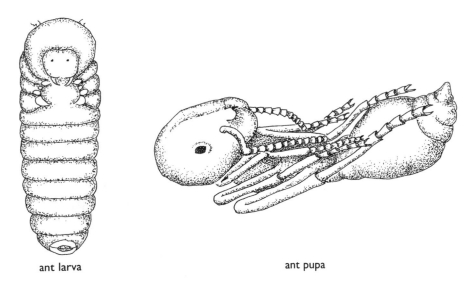

ant larva

ant pupa

An ant passes through the larval and pupal stages of development before it possesses characteristics typical of the mature adult.

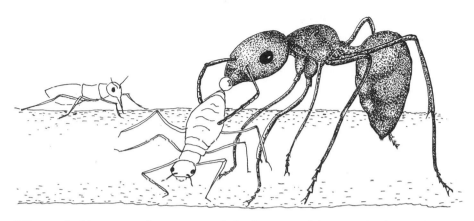

When stroked by an attending ant, an aphid will raise its abdomen and release a droplet of honeydew.

ants appear before long. How long does it take for a group of ants to leave the nest and head for the food? How is the location of the food communicated between ants?

When an ant discovers food during a foraging mission, it chews the food and stores it in its crop. When it returns to the nest, the scout regurgitates some of the stored food into the mouth of another ant. This ant then repeats the exchange with another ant in the colony. In this way the news of a food supply reaches all members of the community within a short time. But how do they find it?

Watch the ant carefully as it returns to the nest. What does it do with the tip of its abdomen as it scurries along? How frequently does the ant do this?

How long does it take for other ants to follow the path of the returning ant?

Rub your finger at right angles across the path of the ant returning to the nest after it has discovered food. What happens to the ants that leave the nest? Describe their behavior. (See Chapter Note 3, on trails.)

CHAPTER NOTES

1. **Ant Antennae.** Antennae are very important in the life of an individual ant and the colony. Antennae are used by an ant to determine whether another ant is from the same colony. Antennae are also used to determine the suitability of food. If you look closely at an antenna, you will see that it is divided into sensory segments from the tip up to the bend in the elbow. The first segment retains the odor of the ant's colony. The second can sense this odor. The third segment is used to follow a trail. The last two segments are for

picking up chemical signals and translating them into care behaviors. From the elbow to the ant's head there are no sensory segments.

2. Ant-Aphid Relationships. Aphids are soft-bodied insects about one-eighth to three-eighths of an inch in length. You can often find aphids feeding on plant leaves with a group of ants in attendance. The ants are seeking the sweet, syrupy honeydew that is a by-product of aphid digestion and is exuded from the aphid intestine. In return for the food, ants offer aphids protection from some of their enemies.

If the ants collecting honeydew from the first group of aphids are from the same colony as the ant you introduce, there will be no noticeable interaction. If the new ant is from a different colony, however, then it will meet with hostility. All foods that are the property of a particular colony are guarded by the ants of that colony.

3. Ant Trails. If more than one ant returns to the nest with evidence of a food source, how do the ants in the nest know which is the best? It seems that not only do ants leave a trail from the food site, but they also leave information about the quality of that food. The frequency of the chemical markings is directly proportional to the success the returning ant had at the site. The number of ants that leave the nest is governed by the concentration of chemicals on the trail.

CHAPTER 16

Earthworms

THE SOIL BUILDERS

Suppose I told you that you could increase the productivity of your garden without using any chemicals. Suppose that I said this product would aerate your soil and improve its water-holding capacity and its texture. It will also neutralize your acidic soil, thus making it hospitable to a greater variety of plants. Interested?

Congratulations! You've just bought a bucket of *Lumbricus terrestris*, also known as earthworms.

You have probably seen many earthworms and you know that they are dull pink, tubelike, slightly pointed at one end, with a series of rings encircling their bodies. But did you know that each of these segments is separated internally by a partition? The earthworm actually resembles a stack of Life Savers. The digestive tract runs from head to tail through the holes in the center of each Life Saver.

The worm's reputation as the gardener's friend is the result of the way this system works. The worm's tiny mouth is at the front end of the worm, usually hidden by a fleshy overhang. When plowing along in loose soil, the worm is selective about what it eats and uses the flap of skin to push aside unsuitable pieces of organic matter and gravel. In more compacted soil the worm can't be as selective. It must literally eat its way through the soil to move around.

As it eats its way along, it leaves a tunnel behind. These tunnels aerate the soil, provide space for growing plant roots, and make canals into which water and nutrients can seep.

The earthworm benefits from the nutrients in the bits of decaying organic matter it eats. In the tunneling process, however, the worm also swallows sand and gravel. Along with food, the gritty material passes from the worm's mouth to its esophagus and then into the crop, or storage chamber, where it remains until muscular contractions move it into the gizzard. In this section of the digestive tract, strong muscular walls expand and contract and, with the help of the gravel, grind the food into smaller pieces.

In the worm's intestines some of this material is broken down into its essential elements, such as nitrogen, phosphorus, oxygen, hydrogen, and sulfur. The animal absorbs whatever it can use and excretes the rest as "casting," a sort of earthworm manure.

The worms often deposit this nutrient-rich material on the soil surface near the entrance to their burrows. The deposits resemble tiny stacks of clay balls. Look for them toward the end of winter and in early spring, when the worms begin to wander aboveground.

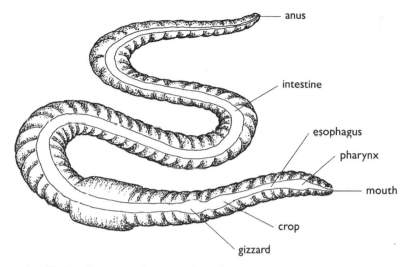

Chemicals added to the material passing through a worm's digestive system neutralize the soil, making acidic and basic soils less so.

The earthworm's agrarian work doesn't stop with soil enrichment. The chemicals it adds to the material passing through the digestive tract neutralize the soil, making acid soils less acidic and basic soils less basic.

If you have ever turned over a spadeful of nutrient-rich garden soil, you have probably seen earthworms in the loose black earth. At first glance you might have thought you had found two different kinds of worms, with fat worms mixed with long thin worms in your scoop of earth. But in fact they are both the same kind of worm. The fat worms are in a state of contraction, and the thin ones are in a state of expansion. The contraction and expansion are a chemical response to being unearthed. Nerve impulses are sent automatically from the earthworm's primitive brain to muscles in each segment of its body.

Alternating expansion and contraction of the muscles propel the worm through the soil, but this is only part of the story. Each segment of the worm's body has four sets of stiff bristles, called setae. Controlled by a separate muscle system, the setae act like anchors to hold the front end of the worm in place as the tail end contracts forward. The worm can also rotate the setae to change the direction of its burrowing. Without these strong hooks the worm would expand and contract without going anywhere. A hungry robin tugging at a worm can attest to the holding power of these tiny anchors.

Pink and eyeless earthworms are ideally suited to the dark, subterranean world, where camouflage is unnecessary and eyesight is useless. Earthworms

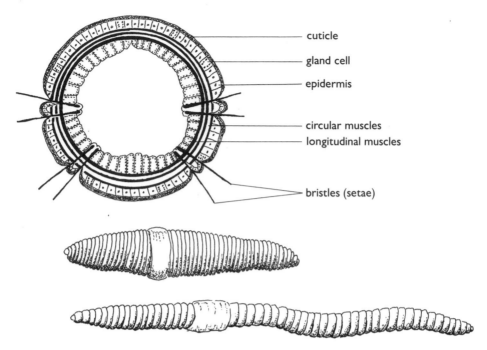

cuticle

gland cell

epidermis

circular muscles

longitudinal muscles

bristles (setae)

Contraction of an earthworm's longitudinal muscles makes it shorter and thicker. Contraction of the circular muscles makes the earthworm longer and thinner.

do have light-sensitive cells scattered over their skin. These light detectors, concentrated near the head, help the worms avoid sunlight. This is important because the ultraviolet radiation of sunlight kills the delicate nerve endings in the skin, which causes paralysis. The worm is only safe from the sun under the soil or beneath the litter that covers the soil.

Earthworms are also earless. Instead, their bodies are covered with tiny nerve endings designed to detect vibrations in the soil. Rumblings or vibrations trigger a series of complex signals. These signals are sent to the worm's brain, warning it of danger, such as hungry moles or slugs, lurking around it in the soil.

Earthworms do not have lungs. Their oxygen needs are met as oxygen from the air is absorbed through the animals' moist skin. The oxygen is then picked up by respiratory pigments, such as hemoglobin. Two major blood vessels extend the length of the worm's body, one along the top and the other along the belly. Blood is pumped throughout the worm's body by five heartlike muscles.

You have probably seen large numbers of earthworms come aboveground after a particularly heavy rainfall. This is because rainwater lacks enough dissolved oxygen to meet the metabolic needs of the worms. Thus, the worms come to the surface seeking oxygen. This is frequently a fatal move for the vulnerable worm.

Earthworms are very busy tillers of the soil, eating their weight every few hours. If the soil is very poor in nutrients, however, it will not support a worm population. If you want to build up the soil in your garden, start by feeding it compost. Then, bring in the worms!

THE WORLD OF EARTHWORMS

What to Bring	Science Skills
basic kit	*observing*
flashlight	*measuring*
large pan	*recording*
paper towels	*comparing*
plastic wrap	
dark cloth	
plastic containers	
2 coffee cans	

OBSERVATIONS

Where to Find Earthworms. Since earthworms thrive on a diet of organic material, one of the best places to find them is in a well-tended garden.

Earthworms cannot survive the ultraviolet rays of the sun, so they have evolved a simple behavioral strategy that reduces their risk of exposure—they generally come aboveground only at night. Use a flashlight in your search. Cover the lens of your flashlight with a piece of red cellophane because a bright, white light signals them to seek shelter. With a dim, red light you'll be able to see them without them seeing you.

You also can find earthworms in the daytime just by digging in your own garden. A shovelful of rich soil will often yield a generous supply of earthworms. Also look for them under leaf litter and decaying logs. Earthworms also squeeze under anything that will shield them from the sun.

You can create earthworm habitat by leaving a short length of wooden plank on the soil in a moist location. Check under the plank after several days. You might have a few worms to add to your collection.

During hot, dry weather you won't find worms close to the surface. They will have tunneled down three feet or so, and are cool and moist in their mucus-coated burrows.

Worms will freeze if the temperature drops below freezing. This is not surprising since earthworms are seventy-five to ninety percent water and have no internal heating system. In freezing temperatures, the worms burrow deeper into the earth where the soil stays about twenty degrees above freezing.

A Closer Look at Earthworms. When you have found some worms, put them into a large flat pan with a thin layer of soil, and begin your investigation simply by observing what they do. Remember an earthworm cannot hurt you, but you can injure it if you don't handle it gently.

Although both ends of a worm look alike at first, they do have a front end and a rear end. Can you tell which is which? What evidence did you use to make your decision?

Make a drawing of your worm. The whitish bandlike structure behind the forward end of the worm is the clitellum, an important part of the worm's reproductive process. (See Chapter Note 1, on reproduction.)

Watch your worms move along on the surface of the soil. Does the shape of the worm change as it moves? If it does, draw the sequence of changes you observe. With your magnifier, look for the bristles on the segments. (See Chapter Note 2, on worm movement.)

Measure your worms. How long are they? Did you measure them when they were long and skinny or when they were short and fat? Are all your earthworms the same length? (See Chapter Note 3 for some interesting earthworm statistics.)

Put a small stone or a twig in front of a moving earthworm. What does the worm do? Put another earthworm in its path. Does it behave differently when it meets another earthworm?

Stroke your worm by running your finger along its back from head to tail. How does it feel? How did the earthworm respond to your touch? What did it do?

EXPLORATIONS

Burrowing. Put an additional two or three inches of soil into your container. Put a worm on top of the soil. How long does it take the worm to burrow out of sight? Try this several times. What is the least amount of time it took a worm to disappear? The most time? The average time? Is the burrowing speed of the worms related to their length? Do larger worms burrow faster than smaller worms?

Reaction to Touch. Put your earthworm on a moist paper towel. With a blunt pencil gently tap various parts of the earthworm body. Which part made the earthworm squiggle the most when you touched it, the head, tail, or

Some earthworms plug the openings of their burrows with pieces of leaves.

middle? Gently poke the clitellum. How does the worm respond? Try these tests with some other earthworms. Do they respond in a similar way?

You might find it helpful to put your discoveries on a chart.

Can you make any generalizations about the sensitivity of the earthworm body to touch?

Response to Light. How do earthworms respond to light? To answer this question you will need two empty coffee cans. You will also need a dark cloth to cover one coffee can and transparent plastic wrap for the other. Put soil in the cans, add a few earthworms to each, and cover them. Check occasionally to find out which worms dug under first.

EARTHWORM REACTIONS TO A GENTLE NUDGE

What You Touched	Worm's Response
head end	
rear end	
clitellum	
back	
underside	

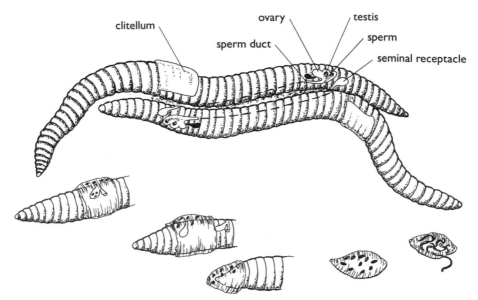

Although each earthworm is capable of fertilizing its own eggs, offspring receive genetic material from two parents. Counterclockwise from top: Earthworms mate and eggs are deposited in the mucous sac that moves back from the clitellum. Sperm are released from the seminal receptacle and fertilization takes place. As the slime sac slips off, its ends close to form a cocoon. The cocoon is deposited near the burrow entrance. Young worms emerge in two to three weeks.

CHAPTER NOTES

1. Earthworm Reproduction. Earthworms are hermaphroditic. This means that each individual can produce male and female sex cells. Most times earthworms mate there is an exchange of sperm from each worm to the other. Since earthworms do not fertilize their own eggs, the offspring receive genetic material from both parents.

After the worms exchange sperm they separate. The clitellum of each worm then produces a slimy sheath that collects the fertilized eggs. A sheath slips off each of the parent worms and is sealed. The parents deposit the sealed sheaths at burrow entrances, where you can occasionally find them. They resemble a kernel of rice.

2. Worm Movement. Earthworms are equipped with two sets of muscles that move the worm through the soil by a series of well-orchestrated expansions and contractions. One set of muscles is called the longitudinal muscles, and they extend the length of the worm's body. The other set is the circular muscles, which wrap around the worm's body.

When the circular muscles in the forward end of the worm contract, the body lengthens and becomes pointed. After this forward push, the setae along the side of the worm body dig in. Then the longitudinal muscles expand, pulling the worm forward. Through the coordination of these muscles and bristles the worms can cover one inch per muscle cycle.

3. Some Earthworm Statistics. Although a mature garden earthworm can be twelve inches long, most of those you find will be smaller, about four to six inches. In the subtropical regions of Brazil there are earthworms as long as twenty feet. These gigantic worms can boast 150 to 250 segments.

Selected Bibliography

THE CANOPY

Asimov, Isaac. *How Did We Find Out About Photosynthesis.* New York: Walker and Company, 1989.

Barkalow, Frederick S., and Monica Shorten. *The World of the Gray Squirrel.* New York: J. B. Lippincott Company, 1973.

Corbo, Margaret. *Arnie the Darling Starling.* Boston: G. K. Hall, 1984.

Hobhouse, Henry. *Seeds of Change: Five Plants That Transformed Mankind.* New York: Harper and Row, 1986.

Hutchins, Ross E. *The Amazing Seeds.* New York: Dodd, Mead, 1965.

Kinkead, Eugene. *Squirrel Book.* New York: E. P. Dutton, 1980.

Kress, Stephen W. *The Audubon Society Handbook for Birders.* New York: Charles Scribner's Sons, 1981.

Peterson, Russell. *The Pine Tree Book.* New York: The Brandywine Press, 1980.

Reich, Lee. "Pines For Eating." *Horticulture* 56 (February 1988): 18-24.

THE FIELD

Bland, John B. *Forests of the Lilliput: The Realm of Mosses and Lichens.* Englewood Cliffs, New Jersey: Prentice Hall, Inc., 1984.

Darwin, Charles. *The Movements and Habits of Hanging Plants,* 2nd ed. revised. New York: D. Appleton & Co., 1897.

Hale, Mason. *How to Know the Lichens.* Dubuque, Iowa: William C. Brown Co., 1969.

Hale, Mason, Jr. *Lichens of California.* San Francisco: University of California Press, 1988.

Shorthouse, J. D., and O. Rohfritsch. *The Biology of Insect-Induced Galls.* New York: Oxford University Press, 1992.

Smith, Richard M. *Wild Plants of America.* New York: John Wiley and Sons, Inc., 1989.

Symonds, Geo. W. D. *The Shrub Identification Book.* New York: Morrow and Co., 1963.

Vitt, Dale H. *Mosses, Lichens, and Ferns of Northwest North America.* Seattle: University of Washington Press, 1988.

THE FOREST FLOOR

Crompton, John. *The Way of the Ant.* New York: Nick Lyons Books, 1989.

Fabre, J. Henri. *The Life of the Spider.* New York: Dodd, Mead, 1913.

Gertsch, W. *American Spiders.* New York: Van Nostrand Reinhold Company, 1979.

Henisch, Bridget. *Chipmunk Portrait.* State College, Pennsylvania: Carnation Press, 1970.

The Journal of Wild Mushrooming: Box 3156, University Station, Moscow, Idaho 83843.

Major, Alan. *Collecting and Studying Mushrooms, Toadstools, and Fungi.* New York: Arco Publishing Company, 1975.

Ordish, George. *The Year of the Ant.* New York: Charles Scribner's Sons, 1978.

Schaller, Friedrich. *Soil Animals.* Ann Arbor: University of Michigan Press, 1968.

Steineck, Hellmut. *Mushrooms in the Garden.* Eureka, California: Mad River Press, 1984.

Tunis, Edwin. *Chipmunks on the Doorstep.* New York: Crowell, 1971.

Wishner, Lawrence Arndt. *Eastern Chipmunks: Secrets of Their Solitary Lives.* Washington, D. C.: Smithsonian Institution Press, 1982.

FIELD GUIDES

Bell, C. Ritchie, and Anne H. Lindsey. *Fall Color Finder.* Chapel Hill, North Carolina: Laurel Hill Press, 1991.

Borror, Donald, and Richard E. White. *Insects: A Field Guide.* Boston: Houghton Mifflin Company, 1970.

Brockman, C. Frank. *Trees of North America.* New York: Golden Press, 1986.

Daniel, Glenda, and Jerry Sullivan. *The Northwoods of Michigan, Wisconsin, Minnesota*. San Francisco: Sierra Club Books, 1981.

Farrand, Jr., John, ed. *The Audubon Society Master Guide to Birding*, vol. 1-4. New York: Alfred Knopf, 1983.

Godfrey, Michael A. *The Piedmont*. San Francisco: Sierra Club Books, 1980.

Harlow, William. *Trees*. New York: Dover Publications, Inc., 1957.

Jorgensen, Neil. *Southern New England*. San Francisco: Sierra Club Books, 1978

Newcomb, Lawrence. *Wildflower Guide*. Boston: Little Brown Co., 1987.

Peterson, Roger Tory, and Margaret McKenny. *A Field Guide to Wildflowers*. Boston: Houghton Mifflin Company, 1962.

Spellenberg, Richard. *Audubon Society Field Guide to North American Wildflowers*. New York: Alfred Knopf, 1979.

GENERAL INTEREST

Chambers, Kenneth A. *A Country Lover's Guide to Wildlife*. Baltimore: John's Hopkins University Press, 1978.

Garland, Trudi H. *Fascinating Fibonaccis: Mystery and Magic in Numbers*. Palo Alto, California: D. Seymour Publications, 1987.

Meeuse, Bastian, and Sean Morris. *The Sex Lives of Flowers*. New York: Facts on File, 1984.

Milne, Lorus, and Margery Milne. *Insect Worlds*. New York: Charles Scribner's Sons, 1980.

Stone, Doris. *The Lives of Plants*. New York: Charles Scribner's Sons, 1984.

NOTES

NOTES

NOTES